PUFFIN BOOKS

THE PUFFIN BOOK OF
TWENTIETH-CENTURY CHILDREN'S VERSE

BRIAN PATTEN was born in Liverpool. His poetry for adults has been translated into many languages, and his collections include *Love Poems, Storm Damage* and *Grinning Jack*. His verse for children includes *Gargling with Jelly* and *Thawing Frozen Frogs*. Brian Patten is a popular performer of his work, and he has written children's plays and the award winning novel, *Mr Moon's Last Case.*

MICHAEL FOREMAN was born in Suffolk. He studied at Lowestoft Art School and then at the Royal College of Art, where he graduated with first class honours. He has worked on magazines, as an illustrator and art director, and in film animation. For twenty years he has also been the art editor of the literary magazine *Ambit*. He is still best known, however, for his work as an author and illustrator of children's books and has been the winner of the Kurt Maschler Award, the Kate Greenaway Medal, the Children's Book Award and twice winner of the Francis Williams Illustration Award. *War Boy* recently won Michael Foreman the Kate Greenaway Medal for the second time.

Michael Foreman spends his time with his wife and sons partly in London and partly at his house in St Ives, Cornwall.

D1041943

The
PUFFIN BOOK *of*
TWENTIETH-CENTURY
CHILDREN'S VERSE

EDITED BY
Brian Patten

ILLUSTRATED BY
Michael Foreman

PUFFIN BOOKS

PUFFIN BOOKS

Published by the Penguin Group
Penguin Books Ltd, 27 Wrights Lane, London W8 5TZ, England
Penguin Putnam Inc., 375 Hudson Street, New York, New York 10014, USA
Penguin Books Australia Ltd, Ringwood, Victoria, Australia
Penguin Books Canada Ltd, 10 Alcorn Avenue, Toronto, Ontario, Canada M4V 3B2
Penguin Books (NZ) Ltd, Private Bag 102902, NSMC, Auckland, New Zealand

On the World Wide Web at: www.penguin.com

Penguin Books Ltd, Registered Offices: Harmondsworth, Middlesex, England

First published by Viking and Puffin 1991
This revised and updated edition published 1999
1 3 5 7 9 10 8 6 4 2

The Acknowledgements on pages 389–396 constitute an extension of this copyright page

The moral right of the illustrator has been asserted

Set in Garamond

Made and printed in England by Clays Ltd, St Ives plc

British Library Cataloguing in Publication Data
A CIP catalogue record for this book is available from the British Library

ISBN 0–140–37684–4

Contents

CONTENTS

CONTENTS

CONTENTS

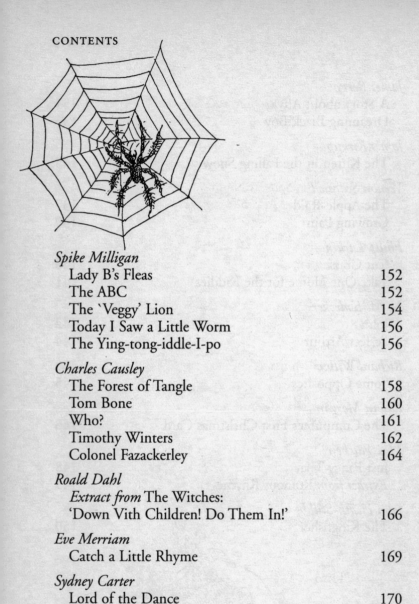

CONTENTS

CONTENTS

CONTENTS

INTRODUCTION

When I told the publishers I didn't think an introduction was necessary for this book they jumped up and down and stamped their feet and fumed and sulked and said, 'You must write one!' When I asked, 'Why?' they looked blank for a moment and then said, 'So you can write about what kind of poems appeal to children.'

'They already know what appeals to them,' I said.

'But what about the adults?' they asked.

'What about them?' I replied. 'I didn't spend ages and ages editing this book for adults, so why should I write an introduction for them?'

But it was no use. They had their hearts set on an introduction, so I sat down and wondered what to write.

And then I suddenly remembered, from a long time ago, a woman called Frieda.

When I was a child I lived in a tiny house that had a front parlour, a kitchen, a main bedroom and a box-room. It was one of many such houses in a maze of terraces that were built before any of the poems in this book were written. The house was shared by three, sometimes four, adults and myself. There was one book in the house. It had a green cover and smelt of moth-balls because for a long time it had lain on the top shelf of a cupboard nobody used. I've forgotten how old I was when I found the book. Perhaps six. I remember wondering what on earth it was doing on top of the cupboard. Did my grandfather have a secret passion for reading? Had he stolen it? Absurdly, that single, harmless book (it was about a fox) filled me with a disproportionate sense of mystery because it was so out of place. Two doors away in an equally small and bookless house lived my aunt, and a few doors beyond her lived Frieda.

The outside of Frieda's house looked no different from the rest and although I never measured the rooms, I'm sure inside it was no bigger than any of the other houses. And yet . . .

There were lots of books in Frieda's house, not arranged

neatly on shelves as if in a library or for show, but scattered all over the place. They were much older than the solitary green book I'd discovered, and they also smelt strange. But not of moth-balls. Some smelt musky but mostly they smelt of bitter coffee, or at least that is how I remember the smell. Frieda's house felt much bigger, and was far more exciting and mysterious than the other houses. I imagined it was bigger because of the books.

When I visited her she would read from, and later, lend me her books. I remember her reading fairy-tales such as The Little Mermaid, and stories like Rip van Winkle.

Frieda's house contained many worlds. It could become a vast coffee-scented cavern in which there were forests to get lost in, it could become an ocean in which mermaids might drown. Her book-filled room contained wolves and snowstorms, mountains and deserts, and in other parts of her dimly lit house people from the books went about their business, released by the magic of imagination from the musky covers that imprisoned them. It was both a frightening and comforting sensation being in her house. Frieda was the last person in our street to change over from gaslight to electricity, and the gas-mantles spluttered, bathing the room in a much gentler and warmer light than the electric bulbs we were getting used to. No other room I had been in was like this book-filled room. In it, I felt free of the restraints imposed on me by adults, it became a sanctuary from the crowded and claustrophobic world in which I lived.

I have tried with this anthology to create a modern version of Frieda's room. A collection of poems is like a room full of books: each poem tells a different story. Some poems remain favourites for life, others rise and fall in our estimation as our tastes change.

Most of the poems in this anthology were written long after the stories in Frieda's books, and there are certainly many funnier, brighter poems here than I ever found among her books. I have tried to gather together some of the best verse written in the English language this century by poets who wrote specially for children. I have also included, though to a lesser extent, work by poets who wrote primarily for adults but whose poems seem to have been adopted by children. Other poems I have included as being worthy of adoption.

I arranged the poems in reverse chronological order because I wanted the book to be a journey back through time. I thought it might be more interesting that way, rather than having the poems scattered all over the place.

While my main source has been individual collections, some poems will be familiar from other anthologies. I saw no point in ignoring a classic like Walter de la Mare's 'The Listeners' as long as I could also include one of his lesser known poems such as 'Tom's Angel'. Some familiar poems were either too good to leave out, or the poet wrote very little else that was suitable for inclusion. It is surprising how many poets whom people think of as 'children's poets' wrote relatively few poems for younger readers. Many thought their work for adults was more important. They were wrong, of course. Take Hilaire Belloc, for example. He was a biographer, historian, essayist and novelist, but if it wasn't for children liking his poems he would be almost forgotten by now.

The first edition of this anthology appeared when there were still nine years of the twentieth century left to run, and since then new poets have appeared whose voices are poised to straddle the twentieth and twenty-first centuries as surely as the voice of Thomas Hardy, the earliest poet represented in this collection, straddled both the nineteenth and twentieth centuries. In order to include them I have omitted a few poems from the earlier edition.

Finally, editing this anthology has confirmed my suspicion that while the majority of poems written for adults seem to age and grow creaky as the years pass, poems written for children retain their freshness. The best have a sense of wonder, mystery and mischief that their older brothers and sisters often seem to lose.

Brian Patten
January 1999

JACKIE KAY

The Frog Who Dreamt She Was an Opera Singer

There once was a frog
who dreamed she was an opera singer.
She wished so hard she grew a long throat
and a beautiful polkadot green coat
and intense opera singer's eyes.
But she couldn't grow tall.
She just couldn't grow tall.
She leaped to the Queen Elizabeth Hall,
practising her sonata all the way.
Her voice was promising and lovely.
She couldn't wait to leapfrog on to the stage.
She had quite a presence on the stage.
All the audience in the Queen Elizabeth Hall,
gasped to see one so small sing like that.
Her voice trembled and swelled
and filled with colour.
The frog was some opera singer.

Word of a Lie

I am the fastest runner in my school and that's
NO WORD OF A LIE
I've got gold fillings in my teeth and that's
NO WORD OF A LIE
In my garden, I've got my own big bull and that's
NO WORD OF A LIE
I'm brilliant at giving my enemies grief and that's
NO WORD OF A LIE
I can multiply three billion and twenty seven by nine
                                                                billion
four thousand and one in two seconds and that's
NO WORD OF A LIE
I can calculate the distance between planets before
                                        you've had toast and that's
NO WORD OF A LIE
I can always tell when my best pals boast and that's
NO WORD OF A LIE
I'd been round the world twice before I was three and a
                                              quarter and that's
NO WORD OF A LIE
I am definitely my mother's favourite daughter and that's
NO WORD OF A LIE
I am brilliant at fake laughter. I go Ha aha Hah ha ha
                                                    and that's
NO WORD OF A LIE
I can tell the weather from one look at the sky and that's
NO WORD OF A LIE

I can predict disasters, floods, earthquakes and murders
and that's

NO WORD OF A LIE
I can always tell when other people lie and that's
NO WORD OF A LIE
I can even tell if someone is going to die and that's
NO WORD OF A LIE
I am the most popular girl in my entire school and that's
NO WORD OF A LIE
I know the golden rule, don't play the fool, don't boast,
don't be shy and that's

NO WORD OF A LIE
I am sensitive, I listen, I have kind brown eyes and that's
NO WORD OF A LIE

You don't believe me do you?
ALLRIGHT, ALLRIGHT, ALL RIGHT
I am the biggest liar in my school and that's
NO WORD OF A LIE

BENJAMIN ZEPHANIAH

This Orange Tree

I touched my first rose
Under this orange tree,
I was young and fruity
The sweet rose was blooming.

I found faith
Under this orange tree
It was here all the time.
One day I picked it up
Then I realized
How great you are.

It was under this
Very orange tree
That I read
My first Martin Luther King speech.
How great the word.

It was here
Under this very orange tree,
On this very peace of earth
That I first sang
With a hummingbird.
How great the song.

This orange tree knows me,
It is my friend,
I trust it and
It taste good.

Body Talk

Dere's a Sonnet
Under me bonnet
Dere's a Epic
In me ear,
Dere's a Novel
In me navel
Dere's a Classic
Here somewhere.
Dere's a Movie
In me left knee
A long story
In me right,
Dere's a shorty
Inbetweeny
It is tickly
In de night.
Dere's a picture
In me ticker
Unmixed riddims
In me heart,
In me texture
Dere's a comma
In me fat chin
Dere is Art.
Dere's an Opera
In me bladder
A Ballad's
In me wrist
Dere is laughter
In me shoulder

In me guzzard's
A nice twist.
In me dreadlocks
Dere is syntax
A dance kicks
In me bum
Thru me blood tracks
Dere run true facts
I got limericks
From me Mum,
Documentaries
In me entries
Plays on history
In me folk,
Dere's a Trilogy
When I tink of three
On me toey
Dere's a joke.

GRACE NICHOLS

A-ra-rat

I know a rat on Ararat,
He isn't thin, he isn't fat
Never been chased by any cat
Not that rat on Ararat.
He's sitting high on a mountain breeze,
Never tasted any cheese,
Never chewed up any old hat,
Not that rat on Ararat.
He just sits alone on a mountain breeze,
Wonders why the trees are green,
Ponders why the ground is flat,
O that rat on Ararat.
His eyes like saucers, glow in the dark –
The last to slip from Noah's ark.

I Like to Stay Up

I like to stay up
and listen
when big people talking
jumbie stories

I does feel
so tingly and excited
inside me

But when my mother say
'Girl, time for bed'

Then is when
I does feel a dread

Then is when
I does jump into me bed

Then is when
I does cover up
from me feet to me head

Then is when
I does wish I didn't listen
to no stupid jumbie story

Then is when
I does wish I did read
me book instead.

RICHARD EDWARDS

The Word Party

Loving words clutch crimson roses,
Rude words sniff and pick their noses,
Sly words come dressed up as foxes,
Short words stand on cardboard boxes,
Common words tell jokes and gabble,
Complicated words play Scrabble,
Swear words stamp around and shout,
Hard words stare each other out,
Foreign words look lost and shrug,
Careless words trip on the rug,
Long words slouch with stooping shoulders,
Code words carry secret folders,
Silly words flick rubber bands,
Hyphenated words hold hands,
Strong words show off, bending metal,
Sweet words call each other 'petal',
Small words yawn and suck their thumbs
Till at last the morning comes.
Kind words give out farewell posies . . .

Snap! The dictionary closes.

Me and Him

'What did you do when you were young?'
I asked of the elderly man.
'I travelled the lanes with a tortoiseshell cat
And a stick and a rickety van,
I travelled the paths with the sun on a thread,
I travelled the roads with a bucket of bread,
I travelled the world with a hen on my head
And my tea in a watering can,
Said the elderly, elderly man.

'And what do you do now that you're old?'
I asked of the elderly man.
'I sit on my bed and I twiddle my thumbs
And I snooze,' he replied, 'and I plan
To make my escape from this nursing-home place
Whose matron is strict with a pale pasty face . . .'
'Then come with me now and away we shall race!'
I said to the elderly man
And he jumped out of bed and we ran.

And now we wander wherever we want,
Myself and the elderly man,
With a couple of sticks and a tortoiseshell cat
And a rickety-rackety van,
We travel the paths with the sun on a thread,
We travel the roads with two buckets of bread,
We travel the world with a hen on each head
And our tea in a watering can,
Young me and the elderly man.

Littlemouse

Light of day going,
Harvest moon glowing,
People beginning to snore,
Tawny owl calling,
Dead of night falling,
Littlemouse opening her door.

Scrabbling and tripping,
Sliding and slipping,
Over the ruts of the plough,
Under the field gate,
Mustn't arrive late,
Littlemouse hurrying now.

Into a clearing,
All the birds cheering,
Woodpecker blowing a horn,
Nightingale fluting,
Blackbird toot-tooting,
Littlemouse dancing till dawn.

Soon comes the morning,
No time for yawning,
Home again Littlemouse creeps,
Over the furrow,
Back to her burrow,
Into bed. Littlemouse sleeps.

When I Was Three

When I was three I had a friend
Who asked me why bananas bend,
I told him why, but now I'm four
I'm not so sure . . .

JOHN AGARD

Don't Call Alligator Long-Mouth Till
You Cross River

Call alligator long-mouth
call alligator saw-mouth
call alligator pushy-mouth
call alligator scissors-mouth
call alligator raggedy-mouth
call alligator bumpy-bum
call alligator all dem rude word
but better wait
        till you cross river.

Limbo Dancer's Soundpoem

Go
down
low
    low
show   low
dem
what
you know
      know
let   know
limb
flow
    flow
      flow
as sound
of drum
grow
    grow
      grow
& body
bend
like bow
    bow
      bow
       limb/bow
        low
         low
          low
           limb/bow

Hatch Me a Riddle

In a little white room
all round and smooth
sits a yellow moon.

In a little white room
once open, for ever open,
sits a yellow moon.

In a little white room,
with neither window nor door,
sits a yellow moon.

Who will break the walls
of the little white room
to steal the yellow moon?

A wise one or a fool?

Laughter's Chant

HA-HA-HA-E-E-E-O
HA-HA-HA-E-E-E-O
HA-HA-HA-E-E-E-O
IN SUNRISE

IN MOONGLOW
I COME I GO

NOW YOU HEAR ME
NOW YOU DON'T.

HA-HA-HA-E-E-E-O
HA-HA-HA-E-E-E-O
HA-HA-HA-E-E-E-O
FROM WIND I COME
TO WIND I GO
IN YOUR EYES
I MAKE RAIN
IN YOUR EYES
I MAKE RAIN.

HA-HA-HA-E-E-E-O
HA-HA-HA-E-E-E-O
HA-HA-HA-E-E-E-O
THUNDER I MAKE ROAR
AT THE DOOR
OF YOUR MOUTH
THUNDER I MAKE ROAR
AT THE DOOR
OF YOUR MOUTH.

HA-HA-HA-E-E-E-O
HA-HA-HA-E-E-E-O
HA-HA-HA-E-E-E-O
ALL RIGHT SAD FACE
I WILL COME AGAIN
TO WRINKLE YOUR NOSE.

MICHAEL DUGAN

Billy

When Billy set his aunt on fire
He squealed with great delight,
'Look how Auntie's burning, Dad.
It makes the room so bright.'

When Billy played at Indians
Other children ran in fright,
For bows and arrows Billy scorned,
Preferring dynamite.

When Dad took Billy to the zoo
He hoped for quiet fun.
His ideas changed when Billy shot
A lion with his gun.

When Billy found a tiger snake
He hit it on the head.
Then took it home to hide it
Inside his grandma's bed.

Obsequious Prawn

Obsequious Prawn
Was very forlorn
And didn't know what to do.

His reason to fret –
He'd been caught in a net
And was heading for somebody's stew.

Nightening

When you wake up at night
And it's dark and frightening,
Climb out of bed
And turn on the lightening.

MICHAEL ROSEN

When You're a Grown-Up

When you're a GROWN-UP
a SERIOUS and SENSIBLE PERSON
When you've stopped being SILLY
you can go out and have babies
and go into a SERIOUS and SENSIBLE shop
and ask for:
Tuftytails, Paddipads, Bikkipegs, Cosytoes
and
Tommy Tippee Teethers.
Sno-bunnies, Visivents, Safeshines
Comfybaths, Dikkybibs
and
Babywipes.
Rumba Rattles and Trigger Jiggers
A Whirlee Three, a Finger Flip
or A Quacky Duck.
And if you're very SENSIBLE
you can choose
Easifitz, Babybuggies and a Safesitterstand.
Or is it a
Saferstandsit?
No it's a Sitstandsafe. I can never remember.
I'm sorry but Babytalk is a very difficult language.
It's for adults only.
Like 'X' films
Much too horrible for children.

I Know Someone Who Can

I know someone who can
take a mouthful of custard and blow it
down their nose.
I know someone who can
make their ears wiggle.
I know someone who can
shake their cheeks so it sounds
like ducks quacking.
I know someone who can
throw peanuts in the air and catch them
in their mouth.
I know someone who can
balance a pile of 12 2p pieces on his elbow
and snatch his elbow from under them
and catch them.
I know someone who can
bend her thumb back to touch her wrist.
I know someone who can
crack his nose.
I know someone who can
say the alphabet backwards.
I know someone who can put their hands in
their armpits and blow raspberries.
I know someone who can
wiggle her little toe.
I know someone who can
lick the bottom of her chin.

I know someone who can
slide their top lip one way
and their bottom lip the other way,
and that someone is
ME.

I'm the Youngest in Our House

I'm the youngest in our house
so it goes like this:

My brother comes in and says:
'Tell him to clear the fluff
Out from under his bed.'
Mum says,
'Clear the fluff
out from under your bed.'
Father says,
'You heard what your mother said.'
'What?' I say.
'The fluff,' he says.
'Clear the fluff
out from under your bed.'
So I say,
'There's fluff under his bed, too,
you know.'
So father says,
'But we're talking about the fluff
under *your* bed.'
'You will clear it up
won't you?' mum says.
So now my brother – all puffed up –
says,
'Clear the fluff
out from under your bed,
clear the fluff
out from under your bed.'

Now I'm angry. I am angry.
So I say – what shall I say?
I say,
'Shuttup Stinks
YOU CAN'T RULE MY LIFE.'

If You Don't Put Your Shoes On Before I Count Fifteen

If you don't put your shoes on before I count fifteen
then we won't go to the woods to climb the chestnut
   one
          But I can't find them
Two
          I can't
They're under the sofa three
          No
          O yes
Four five six
          Stop – they've got knots they've got knots
You should untie the laces when you take your shoes
off seven
          Will you do one shoe while I do the other
          then?
Eight but that would be cheating
          Please
All right
          It always . . .
Nine
          It always sticks – I'll use my teeth
Ten
          It won't it won't
          It has – look.
Eleven
          I'm not wearing any socks

Twelve
        Stop counting stop counting. Mum where
           are my socks mum
They're in your shoes. Where you left them.
        I didn't
Thirteen
        O they're inside out and upside down and
           bundled up
Fourteen
        Have you done the knot on the shoe you
           were . . .
Yes
Put it on the right foot
        But socks don't have right and wrong foot
The shoes silly
Fourteen and a half
        I am I am. Wait.
        Don't go to the woods without me
        Look that's one shoe already
Fourteen and threequarters
        There
You haven't tied the bows yet
        We could do them on the way there
No we won't fourteen and seven eighths
        Help me then
        You know I'm not fast at bows
Fourteen and fifteen sixteeeeenths
        A single bow is all right isn't it
Fifteen we're off
        See I did it.
        Didn't I?

BRIAN PATTEN

The Newcomer

'There's something new in the river,'
The fish said as it swam,
'It's got no scales, no fins, no gills,
And ignores the impassable dam.'

'There's something new in the trees,'
I heard a bloated thrush sing,
'It's got no beak, no claws, no feathers,
And not even the ghost of a wing.'

'There's something new in the warren,'
The rabbit said to the doe,
'It's got no fur, no eyes, no paws,
Yet digs deeper than we can go.'

'There's something new in the whiteness,'
Said the snow-bright polar-bear,
'I saw its shadow on a glacier
But it left no foot-prints there.'

Throughout the animal kingdom
The news was spreading fast –

No beak no claws no feathers,
No scales no fur no gills,
It lives in the trees and the water,
In the earth and the snow and the hills,
And it kills and it kills and it kills.

The Trouble With My Sister

My little sister was truly awful,
She was really shocking,
She put the budgie in the fridge
And slugs in Mummy's stocking.

She was really awful
But it was a load of fun
When she stole Uncle Wilbur's
Double-barrelled gun.

She aimed it at a pork pie
And blew it into bits,
She aimed it at a hamster
That was having fits.

She leapt up on the telly,
She pirouetted on the cat,
She gargled with some jelly
And spat in Grandad's hat.

She ran down the hallway,
She ran across the road,
She dug up lots of earth-worms
And caught a squirming toad.

She put them in a large pot
And she began to stir.
She added a pint of bat's blood
And some rabbit fur.

She leapt up on the Hoover,
Around the room she went.
Once she had a turned-up nose
But now her nose is bent.

I like my little sister,
There is really just one hitch,
I think my little sister
Has become a little witch.

I've Never Heard the Queen Sneeze

I've never heard the Queen sneeze
Or seen her blow her nose,
I've never seen her pick a spot
Or tread on someone's toes,
I've never seen her slide upon
A slippery piece of ice,
I've never seen her frown and say
'This jelly is not nice!'
I've never seen her stick a finger
In her royal and waxy ear,
I've never seen her take it out
And sniff, and say 'Oh dear!'
I've never seen her swop her jewels
Or play frisbee with her crown,
I've never seen her spill her soup
Or drop porridge on her gown.
I wonder what she does
When she sits at home alone,
Playing with her corgies
And throwing them a bone?
I bet they've seen the Queen sneeze
And seen her blow her nose,
I bet they've seen her pick a spot
And tread on someone's toes.
I bet they've seen her slide upon
A slippery piece of ice,
I bet they've seen her frown and say,
'This jelly is not nice!'

I bet they've seen her stick a finger
In her royal and waxy ear,
I bet they've seen her take it out
And sniff and say 'Oh dear!'
I bet they've seen her swop her jewels
And play frisbee with her crown,
I bet they've seen her spill her soup
And drop porridge on her gown.
So why can't I do all these things
Without being sent to bed?
Or failing that, why can't I
Be made the Queen instead?

Squeezes

We love to squeeze bananas,
We love to squeeze ripe plums,
And when they are feeling sad
We love to squeeze our mums.

KIT WRIGHT

Hugger Mugger

I'd sooner be
Jumped and thumped and dumped,

I'd sooner be
Slugged and mugged . . . than *hugged* . . .

And clobbered with a slobbering
Kiss by my Auntie Jean:

You know what I mean:
Whenever she comes to stay,
You know you're bound

To get one.
A quick
  short
  peck
  would
  be
  OK
But this is a
Whacking great
Smacking great
Wet one!

All whoosh and spit
And crunch and squeeze
And '*Dear* little boy!'
And 'Auntie's missed you!'
And 'Come to Auntie, she
Hasn't *kissed* you!'
Please don't do it, Auntie,
PLEASE!

Or if you've absolutely
Got to,

And nothing on *earth* can persuade you
Not to,

The trick
Is to make it
Quick,

You know what I mean?

For as things are,
I really would far,

Far sooner be
Jumped and thumped and dumped,

I'd sooner be
Slugged and mugged . . . than *hugged* . . .

And clobbered with a slobbering
Kiss by my Auntie

Jean!

Laurie and Dorrie

The first thing that you'll notice if
  You meet my Uncle Laurie
Is how, whatever else he does,
  He can't stop saying sorry.

He springs from bed at 5 a.m.
  As birds begin to waken,
Cries, 'No offence intended, lads –
  Likewise, I hope, none taken!'

This drives his wife, my Auntie Dorrie,
  Mad. It's not surprising
She grabs him by the throat and screeches,
  'Stop apologizing!'

My Uncle, who's a little deaf,
  Says, 'Sorry? Sorry, Dorrie?'
'For goodness' sake,' Aunt Dorrie screams,
  'Stop saying sorry, Laurie!'

'Sorry, dear? Stop saying what?'
  'SORRY!' Laurie's shaken.
'No need to be, my dear,' he says,
  'For *no offence is taken.*

Likewise I'm sure that there was none
  Intended on your part.'
'Dear Lord,' Aunt Dorrie breathes, 'what can
  I do, where do I start?'

Then, 'Oh, I see,' says Uncle L.,
  'You mean "stop saying sorry"!
I'm sorry to have caused offence
  Oops! Er . . . *sorry*, Dorrie!'

Just Before Christmas

Down the Holloway Road on the top of the bus
On the just-before-Christmas nights we go,
Allie and me and all of us,
And we look at the lit-up shops below.
Orange and yellow the fruit stalls glow,
Store windows are sploshed with sort-of-snow,
And Santa's a poor old so-and-so,
With his sweating gear and his sack in tow,
And Christ . . . mas is coming!

At the front of the top of the lit-up bus
Way down the Holloway Road we ride,
Allie and me and all of us,
And the butchers chop and lop with pride,

And the turkeys squat with their stuffing inside
By ropes of sausages soon to be fried,
And every door is open wide
As down the road we growl or glide
And Christ . . . mas is coming!

All at the front of the top of the bus,
Far down the Holloway Road we roar,
Allie and me and all of us,
And tellies are tinselled in every store,
With fairy lights over every door,
With glitter and crêpe inside, what's more,
And everyone seeming to say, 'For sure,
Christmas is coming as never before.'
Yes, Christ . . . mas is coming!

Hundreds and Thousands

Under the hair-drier,
Under the hair,

The head of my sister
is dreaming of where

She sits by the sea-shore
On somebody's yacht,

Drinking and thinking
And dreaming of what

She'll buy with her hundreds
And thousands of dollars,

Like ten silver tom-cats
With golden flea-collars

To yawn round the lawn
Of her garden in France

Where she lies by the pool
As the blue ripples dance,

And millions of brilliant
People dive in,

All loaded with money
And honey and gin,

All wonderfully funny
With witty remarks

As the sun in the water
Makes shivering sparks

And there by the pool
She lies browning and basking as

All of the people cry,
'Thank you for asking us!'

That's what I read
in her dopy sea-stare

Under the hair-drier,
Under the hair.

She wakes from her dreaming
Of making a mint

And – *would you believe it?* –
She's UTTERLY SKINT!

She's stealing all *my*
Pocket money from *me*!

'I'm off to the Disco –
Need 20 more p!'

PETER MORTIMER

Babies are Boring

Babies are boring
(Oh yes they are!)
Don't believe mothers
or a doting papa.
Babies are boring
their hands and their bellies,
their pink puffy faces
which wobble like jellies.
Accountants and grandmas
and sailors from Chile
when faced with a baby
act extraordinarily silly.
They grimace and they giggle,
say 'diddle-dum-doo',
they waggle their fingers
(stick their tongues out too).
They slaver and slurp
then they tickle its tummy,
they gurgle and drool:
'Oh, he's just like his mummy!'
'Oh, his mouth is like Herbert's!'
'He's got Uncle Fred's nose!'
'My word, he looks healthy!'
'it's his feed, I suppose?'

Save me from baldness
and the old smell of kippers,
but most of all save me
from all gooey nippers.
I'm a brute, I'm a fiend
and no use to implore me
to tickle its chin,
because all babies bore me.

LIBBY HOUSTON

Talk About Caves

Talk about caves! Tell us,
tell us about them!
What's a cave, what's it like?

'My strongroom, mine,' said the Dragon,
'where I hid my gorgeous gold!'
But he lay gloating there so long,
in the end he turned to stone –
crawl down his twisting throat, you can,
for his breath's quite cold.

'My house once,
whispered the Caveman's ghost.
'O it was good
wrapped in fur by the fire to hear
the roaring beasts in the wood
and sleep sound in earth's arms!
(if you find my old knife there,
you can keep it).'

'My bolthole from the beginning,'
Night said,
'where I've stayed
safe from my enemy, Day.

I watch through a crack the sun
beating away at the door –
"Open up!" he shouts.
He'll never get in!'

'My home, always,' said Water.
'I wash my hands here
and slow as I like I make
new beds to lie on
in secret rooms
with pillows and curtains
and lovely ornaments,
pillars and plumes,
statues and thrones –
what colours the dark hides!
I shape earth's bones.'

'Don't disturb me,' the Bat said.
'This is where I hang my weary head.'

The Dream of the Cabbage Caterpillars

There was no magic spell:
  all of us, sleeping,
dreamt the same dream – a dream
  that's ours for the keeping.

In sunbeam or dripping rain,
  sister by brother
we once roamed with glee
  the leaves that our mother

laid us and left us on,
  browsing our fill
of green cabbage, fresh cabbage,
  thick cabbage, until

in the hammocks we hung
  from the garden wall
came sleep, and the dream
  that changed us all –

we had left our soft bodies,
  the munching, the crawling,
to skim through the clear air
  like white petals falling!

Just so, so we woke –
  so to skip high as towers,
and dip now to sweet fuel
  from trembling bright flowers.

The Old Woman and the Sandwiches

I met a wizened wood-woman
  Who begged a crumb of me.
Four sandwiches of ham I had:
  I gave her three.

'Bless you, thank you, kindly Miss,
  Shall be rewarded well –
Three everlasting gifts, whose value
  None can tell.'

'Three wishes?' out I cried in glee –
  'No, gifts you may not choose:
A flea and gnat to bite your back
  And gravel in your shoes.'

JACK PRELUTSKY

Huffer and Cuffer
(*from* The Sheriff of Rottenshot)

Huffer, a giant ungainly and gruff
encountered a giant called Cuffer.
said Cuffer to Huffer, I'M ROUGH AND I'M TOUGH
said Huffer to Cuffer, I'M TOUGHER.

they shouted such insults as BOOB and BUFFOON
and OVERBLOWN BLOWHARD and BLIMP
and BLUSTERING BLUBBER and BLOATED
                                                    BALLOON
and SHATTERBRAIN, SHORTY and SHRIMP.

then Huffer and Cuffer exchanged mighty blows,
they basted and battered and belted,
they chopped to the neck and they bopped in the nose
and they pounded and pummelled and pelted.

they pinched and they punched and they smacked
             and they whacked
and they rocked and they socked and they smashed,
and they rapped and they slapped and they
             throttled and thwacked
and they thumped and they bumped and they bashed.

they cudgelled each other on top of the head
with swipes of the awfulest sort,
and now they are no longer giants, instead
they both are exceedingly short.

Homework! Oh, Homework!

Homework! Oh, homework!
I hate you! You stink!
I wish I could wash you
away in the sink,
if only a bomb
would explode you to bits.
Homework! Oh, homework!
You're giving me fits.

I'd rather take baths
with a man-eating shark,
or wrestle a lion
alone in the dark,
eat spinach and liver,
pet ten porcupines,
than tackle the homework
my teacher assigns.

Homework! Oh, homework!
You're last on my list,
I simply can't see
why you even exist,
if you just disappeared
it would tickle me pink.
Homework! Oh, homework!
I hate you! You stink!

Today is Very Boring

Today is very boring,
it's a very boring day,
there is nothing much to look at,
there is nothing much to say,
there's a peacock on my sneakers,
there's a penguin on my head,
there's a dormouse on my doorstep,
I am going back to bed.

Today is very boring,
it is boring through and through,
there is absolutely nothing
that I think I want to do,
I see giants riding rhinos,
and an ogre with a sword,
there's a dragon blowing smoke rings,
I am positively bored.

Today is very boring,
I can hardly help but yawn,
there's a flying saucer landing
in the middle of my lawn,
a volcano just erupted
less than half a mile away,
and I think I felt an earthquake,
it's a very boring day.

DENNIS LEE

Lizzy's Lion

Lizzy had a lion
   With a big, bad roar,
And she kept him in the bedroom
   By the closet-cupboard door;

Lizzy's lion wasn't friendly
   Lizzy's lion wasn't tame –
Not unless you learned to call him
   By his Secret Lion Name.

One dark night, a rotten robber
   With a rotten robber mask
Snuck in through the bedroom window –
   And he didn't even ask.

And he brought a bag of candy
   That was sticky-icky-sweet,
Just to make friends with a lion
   (if a lion he should meet).

First he sprinkled candy forwards,
   Then he sprinkled candy back;
Then he picked up Lizzy's piggy-bank
   And stuck it in his sack.

But as the rotten robber
　　Was preparing to depart,
Good old Lizzy's lion wakened
　　With a snuffle and a start.

And he muttered, 'Candy? – piffle!'
　　And he rumbled, 'Candy? – pooh!'
And he gave the rotten robber
　　An experimental chew.

Then the robber shooed the lion,
　　Using every name he knew;
But each time he shooed, the lion
　　Merely took another chew.

It was: 'Down, Fido! Leave, Leo!
　　Shoo, you good old boy!'
But the lion went on munching
　　With a look of simple joy.

It was: 'Stop, Mopsy! Scram, Sambo!
　　This is a disgrace!'
But the lion went on lunching
　　With a smile upon his face.

Then old Lizzy heard the rumble,
　　And old Lizzy heard the fight,
And old Lizzy got her slippers
　　And turned on the bedroom light.

There was robber on the toy-shelf!
  There was robber on the rug!
There was robber in the lion
  (Who was looking rather smug)!

But old Lizzy wasn't angry,
  And old Lizzy wasn't rough.
She simply said the Secret Name:
  '*Lion*! – that's enough.'

Then old Lizzy and her Lion
  Took the toes & tum & head,
And they put them in the garbage,
  And they both went back to bed.

SEAMUS HEANEY

Mid-Term Break

I sat all morning in the college sick bay
Counting bells knelling classes to a close.
At two o'clock our neighbours drove me home.

In the porch I met my father crying –
He had always taken funerals in his stride –
And Big Jim Evans saying it was a hard blow.

The baby cooed and laughed and rocked the pram
When I came in, and I was embarrassed
By old men standing up to shake my hand

And tell me they were 'sorry for my trouble';
Whispers informed strangers I was the eldest,
Away at school, as my mother held my hand

In hers and coughed out angry tearless sighs.
At ten o'clock the ambulance arrived
With the corpse, stanched and bandaged by the
nurses.

Next morning I went up into the room. Snowdrops
And candles soothed the bedside; I saw him
For the first time in six weeks. Paler now,

Wearing a poppy bruise on his left temple,
He lay in the four foot box as in his cot.
No gaudy scars, the bumper knocked him clear.

A four foot box, a foot for every year.

ALLAN AHLBERG

Billy McBone

Billy McBone
Had a mind of his own,
Which he mostly kept under his hat.
The teachers all thought
That he couldn't be taught,
But Bill didn't seem to mind that.

Billy McBone
Had a mind of his own,
Which the teachers had searched for for years.
Trying test after test,
They still never guessed
It was hidden between his ears.

Billy McBone
Had a mind of his own,
Which only his friends ever saw.
When the teacher said, 'Bill,
Whereabouts is Brazil?'
He just shuffled and stared at the floor.

Billy McBone
Had a mind of his own,
Which he kept under lock and key.
While the teachers in vain
Tried to burgle his brain,
Bill's thoughts were off wandering free.

I Did a Bad Thing Once

I did a bad thing once.
I took this money from my mother's purse
For bubble gum.
What made it worse,
She bought me some
For being good, while I'd been vice versa
So to speak – that made it worser.

The Cane

The teacher
had some thin springy sticks
for making kites.

Reminds me
of the old days, he said;
and swished one.

The children
near his desk laughed nervously,
and pushed closer.

A cheeky girl
held out her cheeky hand.
Go on, Sir!

said her friends.
Give her the stick, she's always
playing up!

The teacher
paused, then did as he was told.
Just a tap.

Oh, Sir!
We're going to tell on you,
The children said.

Other children
left their seats and crowded round
the teacher's desk.

Other hands
went out. Making kites was soon
forgotten.

My turn next!
He's had one go already!
That's not fair!

Soon the teacher,
to save himself from the crush,
called a halt.

(It was
either that or use the cane
for real.)

Reluctantly,
the children did as they were told
and sat down.

If you behave
yourselves, the teacher said,
I'll cane you later.

JOHN FULLER

Creatures

The butterfly, alive inside a box,
Beats with its powdered wings in soundless knocks
And wishes polythene were hollyhocks.

The beetle clambering across the road
Appears to find his body quite a load:
My fingers meddle with his highway code

And slugs are rescued from the fatal hiss
Of tyres that kiss like zigzagged liquorice
On zigzagged liquorice, but sometimes miss.

Two snails are raced across a glistening stone
(Each eye thrust forward like a microphone)
So slowly that the winner is unknown.

To all these little creatures I collect
I mean no cruelty or disrespect
Although their day-by-day routine is wrecked.

They may remember their experience,
Though at the time it made no sort of sense,
And treat it with a kind of reverence.

It may be something that they never mention,
An episode outside their apprehension
Like some predestined intervention.

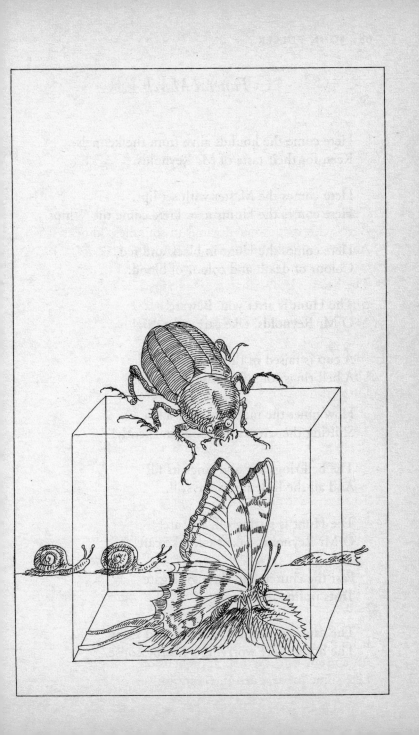

Funeral March

Here come the hounds alive from the kennels,
Keen for their taste of Mr Reynolds.

Here comes the Master with set lips.
Here comes the Huntsman. Here come the Whips.

Here comes the Hunt in black and red,
Colour of death and colour of blood.

The Hunt is after you. Beware!
O Mr Reynolds, take care, take care!

A cup is raised in the village square.
A bell rings roundly through the air.

How quiet the meadows, like a sea
Shifting the wrecks of woods so silently!

The bell rings out and rings its fill
And all the little farms are still.

The Hunt is setting off. Beware!
O Mr Reynolds, take care, take care!

Past the church and through a gate
Trots in line the fox's fate.

The cautious Huntsman slows and stops.
The hounds are worrying a nearby copse.

O Mr Reynolds, were you there?
And left your odour on the air?

The eager hounds from nose to tail
Quiver as they sniff your trail.

They lift their ears, and growl and whine,
Then openly they own the line.

Hear the horn and holloas sing!
Hear the pack's wild yelping ring!

Hear the smallest rider's shout:
Oh they will surely find you out!

The hounds are busy and intent,
Now feathering to chase the scent.

Now the Huntsman's viewed his quarry.
Danger, Mr Reynolds, hurry!

There, there beyond the stream –
A brush of russet tipped with cream.

Now disappearing in the trees,
Padding softly at his ease.

The Hunt is after you. Beware!
O Mr Reynolds, take care, take care!

Lock-Out in Eden

There once was a man with his head full of words
For animals, flowers and fishes and birds.
He lived in a garden with nothing to do
But keep it a-growing and keep himself true.
  Oh Adam, you silly man,
  You were riding for a fall:
  One little apple and you ruined us all.

He wanted a woman, he wanted a friend:
That old temptation, where will it end?
Eve ate the apple and Adam did too.
Together they bit their world in two.
  Oh Adam, you silly man,
  You were riding for a fall:
  One little apple and you ruined us all.

There's a lock-out in Eden, the pickets are there,
A beautiful angel with flaming hair.
He opened the gates and he pushed them through
And now they are mortal like me and you.
  Oh Adam, you silly man,
  You were riding for a fall:
  One little apple and you ruined us all.

Yes, one little apple without permission
Accounts for the whole of the human condition.
East of Eden the family grew
Raising Cain and feeling blue.
  Oh Adam, you silly man,
  You were riding for a fall:
  One little apple and you ruined us all.

ROGER MCGOUGH

Three Rusty Nails

Mother, there's a strange man
Waiting at the door
With a familiar sort of face
You feel you've seen before.

Says his name is Jesus
Can we spare a couple of bob
Says he's been made redundant
And now can't find a job.

Yes I think he is a foreigner
Egyptian or a Jew
Oh aye, and that reminds me
He'd like some water too.

Well shall I give him what he wants
Or send him on his way?
OK I'll give him 5p
Say that's all we've got today.

And I'll forget about the water
I suppose it's a bit unfair
But honest, he's filthy dirty
All beard and straggly hair.

Mother, he asked about the water
I said the tank had burst
Anyway I gave him the money
That seemed to quench his thirst.

He said it was little things like that
That kept him on the rails
Then he gave me his autographed picture
And these three rusty nails.

The Identification

So you think it's Stephen?
Then I'd best make sure
Be on the safe side as it were.
Ah, there's been a mistake. The hair
you see, it's black, now Stephen's fair.
What's that? The explosion?
Of course, burnt black. Silly of me.
I should have known. Then let's get on.

The face, is that a face I ask?
That mask of charred wood
blistered, scarred could
that have been a child's face?
The sweater, where intact, looks
in fact all too familiar.
But one must be sure.

The scoutbelt. Yes that's his.
I recognize the studs he hammered in
not a week ago. At the age
when boys get clothes-conscious
now you know. It's almost
certainly Stephen. But one must
be sure. Remove all trace of doubt.
Pull out every splinter of hope.

Pockets. Empty the pockets.
Handerkchief? Could be any schoolboy's.
Dirty enough. Cigarettes?

Oh this can't be Stephen.
I don't allow him to smoke you see.
He wouldn't disobey me. Not his father.

But that's his penknife. That's his alright.
And that's his key on the keyring
Gran gave him just the other night.
So this must be him.

I think I know what happened
. . . . . . about the cigarettes
No doubt he was minding them
for one of the older boys.
Yes that's it.
That's him.
That's our Stephen.

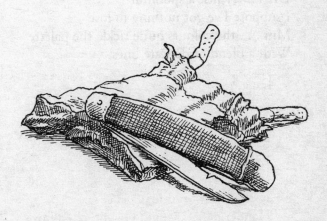

Sky in the Pie!

Waiter, there's a sky in my pie
Remove it at once if you please
You can keep your incredible sunsets
I ordered mincemeat and cheese

I can't stand nightingales singing
Or clouds all burnished with gold
The whispering breeze is disturbing the peas
And making my chips go all cold

I don't care if the chef is an artist
Whose canvases hang in the Tate
I want two veg. and puff pastry
Not the Universe heaped on my plate

OK I'll try just a spoonful
I suppose I've got nothing to lose
Mm . . . the colours quite tickle the palette
With a blend of delicate hues

The sun has a custardy flavour
And the clouds are as light as air
And the wind a chewier texture
(With a hint of cinnamon there?)

This sky is simply delicious
Why haven't I tried it before?
I can chew my way through to Eternity
And still have room left for more

Having acquired a taste for the Cosmos
I'll polish this sunset off soon
I can't wait to tuck into the night sky
Waiter! Please bring me the Moon!

Slug

A 15-amp slug
you are likely to find
in the garden under a rock

Be careful
how you pick it up

You might get
a nasty shock.

Streemin

Im in the botom streme
Which meens Im not brigth
dont like reading
cant hardly write

but all these divishns
arnt reely fair
look at the cemtery
no streemin there

GARETH OWEN

Shed in Space

My Grandad Lewis
On my mother's side
Had two ambitions.
One was to take first prize
For shallots at the village show
And the second
Was to be a space commander.

Every Tuesday
After I'd got their messages,
He'd lead me with a wink
To his garden shed
And there, amongst the linseed
And the sacks of peat and horse manure
He'd light his pipe
And settle in his deck chair.
His old eyes on the blue and distant
That no one else could see,
He'd ask,
'Are we A OK for lift off?'
Gripping the handles of the lawn mower
I'd reply:
'A OK'

And then
Facing the workbench,
In front of shelves of paint and creosote
And racks of glistening chisels
He'd talk to Mission Control.
'Five-Four-Three-Two-One-Zero –
We have lift off.
This is Grandad Lewis talking,
Do you read me?
Britain's first space shed
Is rising majestically into orbit
From its launch pad
In the allotments
In Lakey Lane.'

And so we'd fly,
Through timeless afternoons
Till tea time came,
Amongst the planets
And mysterious suns,
While the world
Receded like a dream:
Grandad never won
That prize for shallots,
But as the captain
Of an intergalactic shed
There was no one to touch him.

Dear Mr Examiner

Thank you so much for your questions
I've read them most carefully through
But there isn't a single one of them
That I know the answer to.

I've written my name as instructed
Put the year, the month and the day
But after I'd finished doing that
I had nothing further to say.

So I thought I'd write you a letter
Fairly informally
About what I can see from my desk here
And what it's like to be me.

Mandy has written ten pages
But it's probably frightful guff
And Angela Smythe is copying
The answers off her cuff.

Miss Quinlan is marking our homework
The clock keeps ticking away
I suppose for anyone outside
It's just another day.

There'll be mothers going on errands
Grandmothers sipping tea
Unemployed men doing crosswords
or watching 'Crown Court' on TV.

The rain has finally stopped here
The sun has started to shine
And in a back garden in Sefton Drive
A housewife hangs shirts on a line.

A class files past to play tennis
The cathedral clock has just pealed
A mower chugs backwards and forwards
Up on the hockey field.

Miss Quinlan's just read what I've written
Her face is an absolute mask
Before she collects the papers in
I've a sort of favour to ask.

I thought your questions were lovely
I've only myself to blame
But couldn't you give me some marks
For writing the date and my name?

NANCY WILLARD

Blake Leads a Walk on the Milky Way

He gave silver shoes to the rabbit
and golden gloves to the cat
and emerald boots to the tiger and me
and boots of iron to the rat.

He inquired, 'Is everyone ready?
The night is uncommonly cold.
We'll start on our journey as children,
but I fear we will finish it old.'

He hurried us to the horizon
where morning and evening meet.
The slippery stars went skipping
under our hapless feet.

'I'm terribly cold,' said the rabbit.
'My paws are becoming quite blue,
and what will become of my right thumb
while you admire the view?'

'The stars,' said the cat, 'are abundant
and falling on every side.
Let them carry us back to our comforts.
Let us take the stars for a ride.'

'I shall garland my room,' said the tiger,
'with a few of these emerald lights.'
'I shall give up sleeping forever,' I said.
'I shall never part day from night.'

The rat was sullen. He grumbled
he ought to have stayed in his bed.
'What's gathered by fools in heaven
will never endure,' he said.

Blake gave silver stars to the rabbit
and golden stars to the cat
and emerald stars to the tiger and me
but a handful of dirt to the rat.

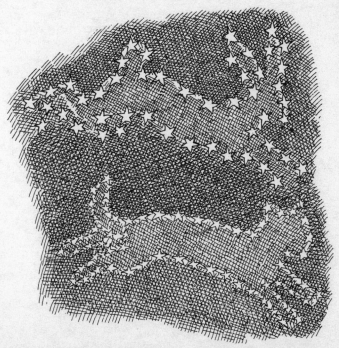

A Rabbit Reveals My Room

When the rabbit showed me my room,
I looked all around for the bed.
I saw nothing there
but a shaggy old bear
who offered to pillow my head.

'I was hoping for blankets,' I whispered.
'At home I've an afghan and sheet.'
You will find my fur soft
as the hay in your loft,
and my paws make an admirable seat.

'I was hoping to waken at sunrise.
At home I've an excellent clock,
a lamp, and a glass
through which the hours pass,
and what shall I do for a lock?'

I will keep you from perilous starlight
and the old moon's lunatic cat.
When I blow on your eyes,
you will see the sun rise
with the man in the marmalade hat.

ADRIAN MITCHELL

Dumb Insolence

I'm big for ten years old
Maybe that's why they get at me

Teachers, parents, cops
Always getting at me

When they get at me

I don't hit em
They can do you for that

I don't swear at em
They can do you for that

I stick my hands in my pockets
And stare at them

And while I stare at them
I think about sick

They call it dumb insolence

They don't like it
But they can't do you for it

Stufferation

Lovers lie around in it
Broken glass is found in it
Grass
I like that stuff

Tuna fish get trapped in it
Legs come wrapped in it
Nylon
I like that stuff

Eskimos and tramps chew it
Madame Tussaud gave status to it
Wax
I like that stuff

Elephants get sprayed with it
Scotch is made with it
Water
I like that stuff

Clergy are dumbfounded by it
Bones are surrounded by it
Flesh
I like that stuff

Harps are strung with it
Mattresses are sprung with it
Wire
I like that stuff

Carpenters make cots of it
Undertakers use lots of it
Wood
I like that stuff

Cigarettes are lit by it
Pensioners get happy when they sit by it
Fire
I like that stuff

Dankworth's alto is made of it, most of it,
Scoobdidoo is composed of it
Plastic
I like that stuff

Apemen take it to make them hairier
I ate a ton of it in Bulgaria
Yoghurt
I like that stuff

Man-made fibres and raw materials
Old rolled gold and breakfast cereals
Platinum linoleum
I like that stuff

Skin on my hands
Hair on my head
Toenails on my feet
And linen on the bed

Well I like that stuff
Yes I like that stuff
The earth
Is made of earth
And I like that stuff

The Woman of Water

There once was a woman of water
Refused a Wizard her hand.
So he took the tears of a statue
And the weight from a grain of sand
And he squeezed the sap from a comet
And the height from a cypress tree
And he drained the dark from midnight
And he charmed the brains from a bee
And he soured the mixture with thunder
And stirred it with ice from hell
And the woman of water drank it down
And she changed into a well.

There once was a woman of water
Who was changed into a well
And the well smiled up at the Wizard
And down down down that old Wizard fell . . .

The Galactic Pachyderm

The elephant stands
among the stars
He jumps off
Neptune
bounces off
Mars
to adventure on
Venus
while his children
play
in the diamond jungles
of the
Milky Way

SYLVIA PLATH

Extract from *The Bed Book*

Beds come in all sizes –
Single or double,
Cot-size or cradle,
King-size or trundle.

Most Beds are Beds
For sleeping or resting,
But the *best* Beds are much
More interesting!

Not just a white little
Tucked-in-tight little
Nighty-night little
Turn-out-the-light little
Bed –

Instead
A Bed for Fishing,
A Bed for Cats,
A Bed for a Troupe of
Acrobats.

The *right* sort of Bed
(If you see what I mean)
Is a Bed that might
Be a Submarine

Nosing through water
Clear and green,
Silver and glittery
As a sardine

Or a Jet-Propelled Bed
For visiting Mars
With mosquito nets
For the shooting stars . . .

ADRIAN HENRI

Tonight at Noon
(for Charles Mingus and the Clayton Squares)

Tonight at noon
Supermarkets will advertise 3p EXTRA on everything
Tonight at noon
Children from happy families will be sent to live in a
                                                    home
Elephants will tell each other human jokes
America will declare peace on Russia
World War I generals will sell poppies in the streets on
                                            November 11th
The first daffodils of autumn will appear
When the leaves fall upwards to the trees

Tonight at noon
Pigeons will hunt cats through city backyards
Hitler will tell us to fight on the beaches and on the
                                            landing fields
A tunnel full of water will be built under Liverpool
Pigs will be sighted flying in formation over Woolton
and Nelson will not only get his eye back but his arm
                                                as well
White Americans will demonstrate for equal rights
in front of the Black House
and the Monster has just created Dr Frankenstein

Girls in bikinis are moonbathing
Folksongs are being sung by real folk
Art galleries are closed to people over 21
Poets get their poems in the Top 20
Politicians are elected to insane asylums
There's jobs for everyone and nobody wants them
In back alleys everywhere teenage lovers are kissing
in broad daylight
In forgotten graveyards everywhere the dead will quietly
bury the living
and
You will tell me you love me
Tonight at noon

Best Friends

It's Susan I talk to not Tracey,
Before that I sat next to Jane;
I used to be best friends with Lynda
But these days I think she's a pain.

Natasha's all right in small doses,
I meet Mandy sometimes in town;
I'm jealous of Annabel's pony
And I don't like Nicola's frown.

I used to go skating with Catherine,
Before that I went there with Ruth;
And Kate's so much better at trampoline:
She's a showoff, to tell you the truth.

I think that I'm going off Susan,
She borrowed my comb yesterday;
I think I might sit next to Tracey,
She's my nearly best friend: she's OK.

SHEL SILVERSTEIN

Jimmy Jet and His TV Set

I'll tell you the story of Jimmy Jet –
And you know what I tell you is true.
He loved to watch his TV set
Almost as much as you.

He watched all day, he watched all night
Till he grew pale and lean,
From 'The Early Show' to 'The Late Late Show'
And all the shows between.

He watched till his eyes were frozen wide,
And his bottom grew into his chair.
And his chin turned into a tuning dial,
And antennae grew out of his hair.

And his brain turned into TV tubes,
And his face to a TV screen.
And two knobs saying 'VERT.' and 'HORIZ.'
Grew where his ears had been.

And he grew a plug that looked like a tail
So we plugged in little Jim.
And now instead of him watching TV
We all sit around and watch him.

The Generals

Said General Clay to General Gore.
'Oh *must* we fight this silly war,
To kill and die is such a bore.'
'I quite agree,' said General Gore.

Said General Gore to General Clay,
'We *could* go to the beach today
And have some ice cream on the way.
'A *grand* idea,' said General Clay.

Said General Clay to General Gore,
'We'll build sand castles on the shore.'
Said General Gore, 'We'll splash and play.'
'Let's go *right now*,' said General Clay.

Said General Gore to General Clay,
'But what if the sea is *closed* today?
And what if the sand's been blown away?'
'A *dreadful* thought,' said General Clay.

Said General Gore to General Clay,
'I've always feared the ocean's spray
And we may drown – it's true, we may,
And we may even drown today.'
'Too true, too true,' said General Clay.

Said General Clay to General Gore,
'My bathing suit is slightly tore,
We'd better go on with our war.'
'I quite agree,' said General Gore.

Then General Clay charged General Gore
As bullets flew and cannon roared.
And now, alas! there is no more
Of General Clay and General Gore.

Sick

'I cannot go to school today,'
Said little Peggy Ann McKay.
'I have the measles and the mumps,
A gash, a rash and purple bumps.
My mouth is wet, my throat is dry,
I'm going blind in my right eye.
My tonsils are as big as rocks,
I've counted sixteen chicken pox
And there's one more – that's seventeen,
And don't you think my face looks green?
My leg is cut, my eyes are blue –
It might be instamatic flue.
I cough and sneeze and gasp and choke,
I'm sure that my left leg is broke –
My hip hurts when I move my chin,

My belly button's caving in,
My back is wrenched, my ankle's sprained,
My 'pendix pains each time it rains.
My nose is cold, my toes are numb,
I have a sliver in my thumb.
My neck is stiff, my spine is weak,
I hardly whisper when I speak.
My tongue is filling up my mouth,
I think my hair is falling out.
My elbow's bent, my spine ain't straight,
My temperature is one-o-eight.
My brain is shrunk, I cannot hear,
There is a hole inside my ear.
I have a hangnail, and my heart is – what?
What's that? What's that you say?
You say today is. . . Saturday?
G'bye, I'm going out to play!'

ALAN BROWNJOHN

Parrot

Sometimes I sit with both eyes closed,
But all the same, I've heard:
They're saying, 'He won't talk because
He is a *thinking* bird.'

I'm olive-green and sulky, and
The family say, 'Oh, yes,
He's silent, but he's *listening*,
He *thinks* more than he says!

'He ponders on the things he hears,
Preferring not to chatter.'
And this is true, but *why* it's true
Is quite another matter.

I'm working out some shocking things
In order to surprise them,
And when my thoughts are ready I'll
Certainly *not* disguise them!

I'll wait, and see, and choose a time
When everyone is present,
And clear my throat and raise my beak
And give a squawk and start to speak
And go on for about a week
And it will not be pleasant!

In Daylight Strange

It was last Friday at ten to four I
Thought of the lion walking into the playground.
I was sitting, thinking, at our table when
The thought of the lion simply came,
And the sun was very hot, and the lion
Was in the yard (in daylight strange, because
Lions go out at night). He was
An enormous, sudden lion and he
Appeared just like that and was crossing very
Slowly the dusty playground, looking
To neither side, coming towards the door. He was
Coloured a yellow that was nearly grey, or a
Grey that was nearly yellow. He was so
Quiet that only I could hear the huge feet
Solidly pacing, and at the playground door he
Stopped, and looked powerfully in. There was
A forest following him, out in the street,
And noises of parakeets. When he stopped,
Looking like a picture of a lion in the frame
Of the open door, his eyes looked on at
Everything inside with a stern, curious look, he
Didn't seem completely to understand. So
He waited a second or two before
He roared. All the reeds on the river bank
Trembled, a thousand feet
Scattered among the trees, birds rose in clouds

But no one jumped in the class-room, no one screamed,
No one ran to ring the firebell, and
Miss Wolfenden went on writing on the board.
It was just exactly as if
They hadn't heard at all, as if nobody had heard.
And yet I had heard, certainly,
Yes. I had heard,
And I didn't jump.
And would you say you were surprised? Because
You ought not to be surprised.
Why should I be frightened when it was
Because *I* thought of the lion, that the lion was there?

TED HUGHES

Leaves

Who's killed the leaves?
Me, says the apple, I've killed them all.
Fat as a bomb or a cannonball
I've killed the leaves.

Who sees them drop?
Me, says the pear, they will leave me all bare
So all the people can point and stare.
I see them drop.

Who'll catch their blood?
Me, me, me, says the marrow, the marrow.
I'll get so rotund that they'll need a wheelbarrow.
I'll catch their blood.

Who'll make their shroud?
Me, says the swallow, there's just time enough
Before I must pack all my spools and be off.
I'll make their shroud.

Who'll dig their grave?
Me, says the river, with the power of the clouds
A brown deep grave I'll dig under my floods.
I'll dig their grave.

Who'll be their parson?
Me, says the crow, for it is well-known
I study the Bible right down to the bone.
I'll be their parson.

Who'll be chief mourner?
Me, says the wind, I will cry through the grass
The people will pale and go cold when I pass.
I'll be chief mourner.

Who'll carry the coffin?
Me, says the sunset, the whole world will weep
To see me lower it into the deep.
I'll carry the coffin.

Who'll sing a psalm?
Me, says the tractor, with my gear grinding glottle
I'll plough up the stubble and sing through my
                                        throttle.
I'll sing the psalm.

Who'll toll the bell?
Me, says the robin, my song in October
Will tell the still gardens the leaves are over.
I'll toll the bell.

Snow and Snow

Snow is sometimes a she, a soft one.
  Her kiss on your cheek, her finger on your sleeve
In early December, on a warm evening,
  And you turn to meet her, saying 'It's snowing!'
    But it is not. And nobody's there.
    Empty and calm is the air.

Sometimes the snow is a he, a sly one.
  Weakly he signs the dry stone with a damp spot.
Waifish he floats and touches the pond and is not.
  Treacherous-beggarly he falters, and taps at the
                             window.
  A little longer he clings to the grass-blade tip
  Getting his grip.

Then how she leans, how furry foxwrap she nestles
  The sky with her warm, and the earth with her
                             softness.
How her lit crowding fairytales sink through the space-
                             silence
  To build her palace, till it twinkles in starlight –
  Too frail for a foot
  Or a crumb of soot.

Then how his muffled armies move in all night
    And we wake and every road is blockaded
Every hill taken and every farm occupied
    And the white glare of his tents is on the ceiling.
        And all that dull blue day and on into the gloaming
    We have to watch more coming.

Then everything in the rubbish-heaped world
    Is a bridesmaid at her miracle.
Dunghills and crumbly dark old barns are bowed in
                            the chapel of her sparkle,
    The gruesome boggy cellars of the wood
        Are a wedding of lace
        Now taking place.

My Other Granny

My Granny is an Octopus
  At the bottom of the sea,
And when she comes to supper
  She brings her family.

She chooses a wild wet windy night
  When the world rolls blind
As a boulder in the night-sea surf,
  And her family troops behind.

The sea-smell enters with them
  As they sidle and slither and spill
With their huge eyes and their tiny eyes
  And a dripping ocean-chill.

Some of her cousins are lobsters
  Some floppy jelly fish –
What would you be if your family tree
  Grew out of such a dish?

Her brothers are crabs jointed and knobbed
  With little pinhead eyes,
Their pincers crack the biscuits
  And they bubble joyful cries.

Crayfish the size of ponies
  Creak as they sip their milk.
My father stares in horror
  At my mother's secret ilk.

They wave long whiplash antennae,
   They sizzle and they squirt –
We smile and waggle our fingers back
   Or grandma would be hurt.

'What's new, Ma?' my father asks,
   'Down in the marvellous deep?'
Her face swells up, her eyes bulge huge
   And she begins to weep.

She knots her sucker tentacles
   And gapes like a nestling bird,
And her eyes flash, changing stations,
   As she attempts a WORD

Then out of her eyes there brim two drops
   That plop into her saucer –
And that is all she manages,
   And my Dad knows he can't force her.

And when they've gone, my ocean-folk,
   No man could prove they came –
For the sea-tears in her saucer
   And a man's tears are the same.

Horrible Song

The Crow is a wicked creature
   Crooked in every feature.
Beware, beware of the Crow!
When the bombs burst, he laughs, he shouts;
When guns go off, he roundabouts;
When the limbs start to fly and the blood starts to flow
   Ho Ho Ho
   He sings the Song of the Crow.

The Crow is a sudden creature
   Thievish in every feature.
Beware, beware of the Crow!
When the sweating farmers sleep
He levers the jewels from the heads of their sheep.
Die in a ditch, your own will go,
   Ho Ho Ho
   While he sings the Song of the Crow.

The Crow is a subtle creature
   Cunning in every feature.
Beware, beware of the Crow!
When sick folk tremble on their cots
He sucks their souls through the chimney pots,
They're dead and gone before they know,
   Ho Ho Ho
   And he sings the Song of the Crow.

The crow is a lusty creature
   Gleeful in every feature.
Beware, beware of the Crow!
If he can't get your liver, he'll find an old rat
Or highway hedgehog hammered flat,
Any old rubbish to make him grow,
   Ho Ho Ho
     While he sings the Song of the Crow.

The crow is a hardy creature
   Fire-proof in every feature.
Beware, beware of the Crow!
When Mankind's blasted to kingdom come
The Crow will dance and hop and drum
And into an old thigh-bone he'll blow
   Ho Ho Ho
     Singing the Song of the Crow.

Amulet

Inside the wolf's fang, the mountain of heather.
Inside the mountain of heather, the wolf's fur.
Inside the wolf's fur, the ragged forest.
Inside the ragged forest, the wolf's foot.
Inside the wolf's foot, the stony horizon.
Inside the stony horizon, the wolf's tongue.
Inside the wolf's tongue, the doe's tears.
Inside the doe's tears, the frozen swamp.
Inside the frozen swamp, the wolf's blood.
Inside the wolf's blood, the snow wind.
Inside the snow wind, the wolf's eye.
Inside the wolf's eye, the North star.
Inside the North star, the wolf's fang.

MARY ANN HOBERMAN

Whale

A whale is stout about the middle,
He is stout about the ends,
& so is all his family
& so are all his friends.

He's pleased that he's enormous,
He's happy he weighs tons,
& so are all his daughters
& so are all his sons.

He eats when he is hungry
Each kind of food he wants,
& so do all his uncles
& so do all his aunts.

He doesn't mind his blubber,
He doesn't mind his creases,
& neither do his nephews
& neither do his nieces.

You may find him chubby,
You may find him fat,
But he would disagree with you:
He likes himself like that.

Combinations

A flea flew by a bee. The bee
To flee the flea flew by a fly.
The fly flew high to flee the bee
Who flew to flee the flea who flew
To flee the fly who now flew by.

The bee flew by the fly. The fly
To flee the bee flew by the flea.
The flea flew high to flee the fly
Who flew to flee the bee who flew
To flee the flea who now flew by.

The fly flew by the flea. The flea
To flee the fly flew by the bee.
The bee flew high to flee the flea
Who flew to flee the fly who flew
To flee the bee who now flew by.

The flea flew by the fly. The fly
To flee the flea flew by the bee.
The bee flew high to flee the fly
Who flew to flee the flea who flew
To flee the bee who now flew by.

The fly flew by the bee. The bee
To flee the fly flew by the flea.
The flea flew high to flee the bee
Who flew to flee the fly who flew
To flee the flea who now flew by.

The bee flew by the flea. The flea
To flee the bee flew by the fly.
The fly flew high to flee the flea
Who flew to flee the bee who flew
To flee the fly who now flew by.

Brother

I had a little brother
And I brought him to my mother
And I said I want another
Little brother for a change.

But she said don't be a bother
So I took him to my father
And I said this little bother
Of a brother's very strange.

But he said one little brother
Is exactly like another
And every little brother
Misbehaves a bit, he said.

So I took the little bother
From my mother and my father
And I put the little bother
Of a brother back to bed.

CHRISTOPHER LOGUE

The Ass's Song

In a nearby town
there lived an Ass,

who in this life
(as all good asses do)

helped his master,
loved his master,

served his master,
faithfully and true.

Now the good Ass worked
the whole day through,

from dawn to dusk
(and on his Sundays, too)

so the master knew
as he rode to mass

God let him sit
on the perfect Ass.

When the good Ass died
and fled above

for his reward
(that all good asses have)

his master made
from his loyal hide

a whip with which
his successor was lashed.

ELIZABETH JENNINGS

The Secret Brother

Jack lived in the green-house
When I was six,
With glass and with tomato plants,
Not with slates and bricks.

I didn't have a brother,
Jack became mine.
Nobody could see him,
He never gave a sign.

Just beyond the rockery,
By the apple-tree,
Jack and his old mother lived,
Only for me.

With a tin telephone
Held beneath the sheet,
I would talk to Jack each night.
We would never meet.

Once my sister caught me,
Said, 'He isn't there.
Down among the flower-pots
Cramm the gardener

Is the only person.'
I said nothing, but
Let her go on talking.
Yet I moved Jack out.

He and his old mother
Did a midnight flit.
No one knew his number:
I had altered it.

Only I could see
The sagging washing-line
And my brother making
Our own secret sign.

The Rabbit's Advice

I have been away too long.
Some of you think I am only a nursery tale,
One of which you've grown out of.
Or perhaps you saw a movie and laughed at my ears
But rather envied my carrot.
I must tell you that I exist.

I'm a puff of wool leaping across a field,
Quick to all noises,
Smelling my burrow of safety.
I am easily frightened. A bird
Is tame compared to me.
Perhaps you have seen my fat white cousin who sits,
Constantly twitching his nose,
Behind bars in a hutch at the end of a garden.
If not, imagine those nights when you lie awake
Afraid to turn over, afraid
Of night and dawn and sleep.
Terror is what I am made
Of partly, partly of speed.

But I am a figure of fun.
I have no dignity
Which means I am never free.
So, when you are frightened or being teased, think of
My twitching whiskers, my absurd white puff of a tail,
Of all that I mean by 'me'
And my ludicrous craving for love.

Lullaby

Sleep, my baby, the night is coming soon.
Sleep, my baby, the day has broken down.

Sleep now: let silence come, let the shadows form
A castle of strength for you, a fortress of calm.

You are so small, sleep will come with ease.
Hush now, be still now, join the silences.

RAYMOND WILSON

Never Since Eden

The Thing that came from Outer Space
And landed in the Jones' backyard
Had neither colour, size nor shape,
But a smell that caught us all off guard.

Never since Eden had there been
So sweet, so rich, so good a smell:
The neighbours, sniffing, gathered round
Like thirsting cattle at a well.

Never since Adam first kissed Eve
Had humans looked upon each other
With such joy that old enemies
Threw loving arms round one another.

One whiff, and babies stopped their crying,
And all the gossip was kind and good,
And thieves and thugs and hooligans
Danced in the street in holiday mood.

Old scores were settled with a smile,
And liars changed to honest men,
And the ugliest face was beautiful,
And the sick and infirm were made whole again.

The Thing that came from Outer Space
Purred like a cat at the heart of the smell,
But how it did, and why it did,
Was more than the Scientists could tell.

They roped it off, they cleared the streets,
They closed upon it, wearing masks,
Ringed it with Geiger counters, scooped
And sealed it in aseptic flasks.

They took it back to analyse
In laboratories white and bare,
And they proved with burette and chromatograph
That nothing whatever was there.

They sterilized the Jones' backyard
(The smell whimpered and died without trace),
Then they showed by mathematics that no Thing
Could have landed from Outer Space.

So the neighbours are quite their old selves now,
As loving as vipers or stoats,
Cheating and lying and waiting their chance
To leap at each other's throats.

RUSSELL HOBAN

Funeral

Gloria and I have often,
Walking slowly, singing steady,
With a shoebox for a coffin,
Buried neighbours who were ready.

Harold Woodmouse, Bertha Toad
(One a cat killed, one a dog)
On the hillside near the road
Sleep along with Herman Frog.

In our funeral today,
Going to his final rest:
Buster William Henry Jay,
Fallen lately from the nest.

Not quite old enough to fly,
Barely big enough to die –
In the hillside here we lay
Buster William Henry Jay.

JAMES BERRY

A Story about Afiya

Afiya has fine black skin
that shows off her white clothes
and big brown eyes that laugh
and long limbs that play.
She has a white summer frock
she wears and washes every night
that every day picks on something
to collect, strangely.

Afiya passes sunflowers and finds
the yellow fringed black faces there,
imprinted on her frock, all over.
Another time she passes red roses
and there the clustered bunches
are, imprinted on her frock.

She walks through high grass and sees
butterflies and all kinds
of slender stalks and petals
patterned on her back and front
and are still there, after
she has washed her dress.

Afiya stands. She watches
the sharp pictures in colour,
untouched by her wash.
Yet, next morning, every day,
the dress is cleared and ready,
hanging white as new paper.

Then pigeons fly up before her
and decorate her dress
with their flight and group design.
Afiya goes to the zoo;
she comes back with two tigers
together, on her back and on her front.

She goes to the seaside;
she comes home with fishes
under ruffled waves
in the whole stretch of sea
imprinted on her dress.

She walks between round and towered
boulders and takes them away,
pictured on her.

Always Afiya is amazed,
just like when she comes home
and finds herself covered
with windswept leaves
of October, falling.

Afiya: a Swahili name meaning health, is pronounced Ah-fee-yah

Dreaming Black Boy

I wish my teacher's eyes wouldn't
go past me today. Wish he'd know
it's okay to hug me when I kick
a goal. Wish I myself wouldn't
hold back when an answer comes.
I'm no woodchopper now
like all ancestors.

I wish I could be educated
to the best of tune up, and earn
good money and not sink to lick
boots. I wish I could go on every
crisscross way of the globe
and no persons or powers or
hotel keepers would make it a waste.

I wish life wouldn't spend me out
opposing. Wish same way creation
would have me stand it would have
me stretch, and hold high, my voice
Paul Robeson's, my inside eye
a sun. Nobody wants to say
hello to nasty answers.

I wish torch throwers of night
would burn lights for decent times.
Wish plotters in pyjamas would pray
for themselves. Wish people wouldn't
talk as if I dropped from Mars.

I wish only boys were scared
behind bravados, for I could suffer
I could suffer a big big lot.
I wish nobody would want to earn
the terrible burden I can suffer.

JAMES KIRKUP

The Kitten in the Falling Snow

The year-old kitten
has never seen snow,
fallen or falling, until now
this late winter afternoon.

He sits with wide eyes
at the firelit window, sees
white things falling
from black trees.

Are they petals, leaves or birds?
They cannot be the cabbage whites
he batted briefly with his paws,
or the puffball seeds in summer grass.

They make no sound, they have no wings
and yet they can whirl and fly around
until they swoop like swallows, and
disappear into the ground.

'Where do they go?' he questions,
with eyes ablaze, following their flight
into black stone. So I put him
out into the yard, to make their acquaintance.

He has to look up at them: when one
blanches his coral nose, he sneezes,
and flicks a few from his whiskers, from
his sharpened ear, that picks up silences.

He catches one on a curled-up paw
and licks it quickly, before
its strange milk fades, then sniffs its ghost,
a wetness, while his black coat

shivers with stars of flickering frost.
He shivers at something else that makes his thin
tail swish, his fur stand on end! 'What's this? . . .'
Then he suddenly scoots in to safety

and sits again with wide eyes
at the firelit window, sees
white things falling
from black trees.

VERNON SCANNELL

The Apple-Raid

Darkness came early, though not yet cold;
Stars were strung on the telegraph wires;
Street lamps spilled pools of liquid gold;
The breeze was spiced with garden fires.

That smell of burnt leaves, the early dark,
Can still excite me but not as it did
So long ago when we met in the park –
Myself, John Peters and David Kidd.

We moved out of town to the district where
The lucky and wealthy had their homes
With garages, gardens, and apples to spare
Ripely clustered in the trees' green domes.

We chose the place we meant to plunder
And climbed the wall and dropped down to
The secret dark. Apples crunched under
Our feet as we moved through the grass and dew.

The clusters on the lower boughs of the tree
Were easy to reach. We stored the fruit
In pockets and jerseys until all three
Boys were heavy with their tasty loot.

Safe on the other side of the wall
We moved back to town and munched as we went.
I wonder if David remembers at all
That little adventure, the apples' fresh scent.

Strange to think that he's fifty years old,
That tough little boy with scabs on his knees;
Stranger to think that John Peters lies cold
In an orchard in France beneath apple trees.

Growing Pain

The boy was barely five years old.
We sent him to the little school
And left him there to learn the names
Of flowers in jam jars on the sill
And learn to do as he was told.
He seemed quite happy there until
Three weeks afterwards, at night,
The darkness whimpered in his room.
I went upstairs, switched on his light,
And found him wide awake, distraught,
Sheets mangled and his eiderdown
Untidy carpet on the floor.
I said, 'Why can't you sleep? A pain?'
He snuffled, gave a little moan,
And then he spoke a single word:
'Jessica.' The sound was blurred.
'Jessica? What do you mean?'
'A girl at school called Jessica,
She hurts –' he touched himself between
The heart and stomach '– she has been
Aching here and I can see her.'
Nothing I had read or heard
Instructed me in what to do.
I covered him and stroked his head.
'The pain will go, in time,' I said.

PHILIP LARKIN

Cut Grass

Cut grass lies frail:
Brief is the breath
Mown stalks exhale.
Long, long the death

It dies in the white hours
Of young-leafed June
With chestnut flowers,
With hedges snowlike strewn,

White lilac bowed,
Lost lanes of Queen Anne's lace,
And that highbuilded cloud
Moving at summer's pace.

Take One Home for the Kiddies

On shallow straw, in shadeless glass,
Huddled by empty bowls, they sleep:
No dark, no dam, no earth, no grass –
Mam, get us one of them to keep.

Living toys are something novel,
But it soon wears off somehow.
Fetch the shoebox, fetch the shovel –
Mam, we're playing funerals now.

N. M. BODECKER

John

John could take his clothes off
but could not put them on.

His patient mother dressed him,
and said to little John,

'Now, John! You keep your things on.'
But John had long since gone –

and left a trail of sneakers
and small things in the sun,

so she would know to find him
wherever he might run.

And at the end of every trail
stood Mrs Jones & Son,

she with all his little clothes,
and little John with none!

For John could take his clothes off
but could not put them on.

His patient mother dressed him
and on went little John –
and on –
　　　and on –
　　　　　and on –

Perfect Arthur

'Nowhere in the world,'
said Arthur,
'nowhere in the world,'
said he,
'is a boy
as absolutely
*per*fectly
perfect
as me!'

'Or, on second thought,'
said Arthur,
as he caught his mother's eye,
'should I say,
as absolutely
*per*fectly
perfect
as I?'

RICHARD WILBUR

Some Opposites

What is the opposite of *riot*?
It's *lots of people keeping quiet.*

The opposite of *doughnut*? Wait
A minute while I meditate.
This isn't easy. Ah, I've found it!
A cookie with a hole around it.

What is the opposite of *two*?
A lonely me, a lonely you.

The opposite of a *cloud* could be
A white reflection in the sea,
Or a huge blueness in the air,
Caused by a cloud's not being there.

The opposite of *opposite*?
That's much too difficult. I quit.

EDWIN MORGAN

The Computer's First Christmas Card

jollymerry
hollyberry
jollyberry
merryholly
happyjolly
jollyjelly
jellybelly
bellymerry
hollyheppy
jollyMolly
marryJerry
merryHarry
happyBarry
heppyJarry
boppyheppy
berryjorry
jorryjolly
moppyjelly
Mollymerry
Jerryjolly
bellyboppy
jorryhoppy
hollymoppy
Barrymerry
Jarryhappy

happyboppy
boppyjolly
jollymerry
merrymerry
merrymerry
merryChris
ammerryasa
Chrismerry
asMERRYCHR
YSANTHEMUM

MAX FATCHEN

Just Fancy That

'Just fancy that!' my parents say
At anything I mention.
They always seem so far away
And never pay attention.

'Just fancy that,' their eyes are glazed.
It grows so very wearing.
'Just fancy that' is not a line
For which I'm really caring.

And so today I'm telling them
I threw a cricket bat.
I broke a windowpane at school.
They murmur, 'Fancy that.'

I wrote a message on the fence.
I spoke a wicked word.
The way the vicar hurried past,
I'm positive he heard.

'Just fancy that.' Then suddenly
Their eyes are sticking out,
Their words are coming in a rush
Their voices in a shout.

'You naughty child, you shameless boy,
It's time WE had a chat.'
Hurrah, they've noticed me at last.
My goodness, fancy that!

Extract from *Ruinous Rhymes*

Pussycat, pussycat, where have you been,
Licking your lips with your whiskers so clean?
Pussycat, pussycat, purring and pudgy,
Pussycat, pussycat. WHERE IS OUR BUDGIE?

JOHN HEATH-STUBBS

The Kingfisher

When Noah left the Ark, the animals
Capered and gambolled on the squadgy soil,
Enjoying their new-found freedom; and the birds
Soared upwards, twittering, to the open skies.

But one soared higher than the rest, in utter ecstasy,
Till all his back and wings were drenched
With the vivid blue of heaven itself, and his breast
                                                scorched
With the upward-slanting rays of the setting sun.
When he came back to earth, he had lost the Ark;
His friends were all dispersed. So now he soars no
                                                more;
A lonely bird, he darts and dives for fish,
By streams and pools – places where water is –
Still searching, but in vain, for the vanished Ark
And rain-washed terraces of Ararat.

SPIKE MILLIGAN

Lady B's Fleas

Lady Barnaby takes her ease
   Knitting overcoats for fleas
By this kindness, fleas are smitten
   That's why she's very rarely bitten.

The ABC

T'was midnight in the schoolroom
And every desk was shut,
When suddenly from the alphabet
Was heard a loud 'Tut-tut!'

Said A to B, 'I don't like C;
His manners are a lack.
For all I ever see of C
Is a semi-circular back!'

'I disagree,' said D to B,
'I've never found C so.
From where *I* stand, he seems to be
An uncompleted O.'

C was vexed, 'I'm much perplexed,
You criticize my shape.
I'm made like that, to help spell Cat
And Cow and Cool and Cape.'

'He's right,' said E; said F, 'Whoopee!'
Said G, ''Ip, 'ip, 'ooray!'
'You're dropping me,' roared H to G.
'Don't do it please I pray!'

'Out of my way,' LL said to K.
'I'll make poor I look ILL.'
To stop this stunt, J stood in front,
And presto! ILL was JILL.

'U know,' said V, 'that W
Is twice the age of me,
For as a Roman V is five
I'm half as young as he.'

X and Y yawned sleepily,
'Look at the time!' they said.
'Let's all get off to beddy byes.'
They did, then, 'Z-z-z.'

or
alternative last verse

X and Y yawned sleepily,
'Look at the time!' they said.
They all jumped in to beddy byes
And the last one in was Z!'

The 'Veggy' Lion

I'm a vegetarian Lion,
I've given up all meat,
I've given up all roaring
All I do is go tweet-tweet.

I never ever sink my claws
Into some animal's skin,
It only lets the blood run out
And lets the germs rush in.

I used to be ferocious,
I even tried to kill!
But the sight of all that blood
made me feel quite ill.

I once attacked an Elephant
I sprang straight at his head.
I woke up three days later
In a Jungle hospital bed.

Now I just eat carrots,
They're easier to kill,
'Cos when I pounce upon them,
They all remain quite still!

Today I Saw a Little Worm

Today I saw a little worm
Wriggling on his belly.
Perhaps he'd like to come inside
And see what's on the Telly.

The Ying-tong-iddle-I-po

My Uncle Jim-jim
Had for years
Suffered from
Protruding ears.

Each morning then,
When he got up,
They stuck out like handles
on the F.A. Cup.

He tied them back
With bits of string
But they shot out again
With a noisy – *PING*!

They flapped in the wind
And in the rain,
Filled up with water
Then emptied again.

One morning Jim-jim
Fell out of bed
and got a Po
Stuck on his head.

He gave a Whoop,
A happy shout,
His ears no longer now
Stuck out.

For the rest of his days
He wore that Po,
But now at night
He has nowhere to go.

CHARLES CAUSLEY

The Forest of Tangle

Deep in the Forest of Tangle
The King of the Makers sat
With a faggot of stripes for the tiger
And a flitter of wings for the bat.

He'd teeth and he'd claws for the cayman
And barks for the foxes and seals,
He'd a grindstone for sharpening swordfish
And electrical charges for eels.

He'd hundreds of kangaroo-pouches
On bushes and creepers and vines,
He'd hoots for the owls and for glow-worms
He'd goodness knows how many shines.

He'd bellows for bullfrogs in dozens
And rattles for snakes by the score,
He'd hums for the humming-birds, buzzes for bees,
And elephant trumpets galore.

He'd pectoral fins for sea-fishes
With which they might glide through the air,
He'd porcupine quills and a bevy of bills
And various furs for the bear.

But O the old King of the Makers
With tears could have filled up a bay,
For no one had come to his warehouse
These many long years and a day.

And sadly the King of the Makers
His bits and his pieces he eyed
As he sat on a rock in the midst of his stock
And he cried and he cried and he cried.
He cried and he cried and he cried and he cried,
He cried and he cried and he cried.

Tom Bone

My name is Tom Bone,
I live all alone
In a deep house on Winter Street.
　　Through my mud wall
　　The wolf-spiders crawl
　　And the mole has his beat.

On my roof of green grass
All the day footsteps pass
In the heat and the cold,
　　As snug in a bed
　　With my name at its head
　　One great secret I hold.

Tom Bone, when the owls rise
In the drifting night skies
Do you walk round about?
　　All the solemn hours through
　　I lie down just like you
　　And sleep the night out.

Tom Bone, as you lie there
On your pillow of hair,
What grave thoughts do you keep?
　　Tom says, 'Nonsense and stuff!
　　You'll know soon enough.
　　Sleep, darling, sleep.'

Who?

Who is that child I see wandering, wandering
Down by the side of the quivering stream?
Why does he seem not to hear, though I call to him?
Where does he come from, and what is his name?

Why do I see him at sunrise and sunset
Taking, in old-fashioned clothes, the same track?
Why, when he walks, does he cast not a shadow
Though the sun rises and falls at his back?

Why does the dust lie so thick on the hedgerow
By the great field where a horse pulls the plough?
Why do I see only meadows, where houses
Stand in a line by the riverside now?

Why does he move like a wraith by the water,
Soft as the thistledown on the breeze blown?
When I draw near him so that I may hear him,
Why does he say that his name is my own?

Timothy Winters

Timothy Winters comes to school
With eyes as wide as a football pool,
Ears like bombs and teeth like splinters:
A blitz of a boy is Timothy Winters.

His belly is white, his neck is dark,
And his hair is an exclamation mark.
His clothes are enough to scare a crow
And through his britches the blue winds blow.

When teacher talks he won't hear a word
And he shoots down dead the arithmetic-bird,
He licks the patterns off his plate
And he's not even heard of the Welfare State.

Timothy Winters has bloody feet
And he lives in a house on Suez Street,
He sleeps in a sack on the kitchen floor
And they say there aren't boys like him any more.

Old Man Winters likes his beer
And his missus ran off with a bombardier,
Grandma sits in the grate with a gin
And Timothy's dosed with an aspirin.

The Welfare Worker lies awake
But the law's as tricky as a ten-foot snake,
So Timothy Winters drinks his cup
And slowly goes on growing up.

At Morning Prayers the Master helves
For children less fortunate than ourselves,
And the loudest response in the room is when
Timothy Winters roars 'Amen!'

So come one angel, come on ten:
Timothy Winters says 'Amen
Amen amen amen amen.'
Timothy Winters, Lord.
  Amen.

helves: a dialect word from north Cornwall used to describe the alarmed lowing of
cattle (as when a cow is separated from her calf); a desperate, pleading note

Colonel Fazackerley

Colonel Fazackerley Butterworth-Toast
Bought an old castle complete with a ghost,
But someone or other forgot to declare
To Colonel Fazack that the spectre was there.

On the very first evening, while waiting to dine,
The Colonel was taking a fine sherry wine,
When the ghost, with a furious flash and a flare,
Shot out of the chimney and shivered, 'Beware!'

Colonel Fazackerley put down his glass
And said, 'My dear fellow, that's really first class!
I just can't conceive how you do it at all.
I imagine you're going to a Fancy Dress Ball?'

At this, the dread ghost gave a withering cry.
Said the Colonel (his monocle firm in his eye),
'Now just how you do it I wish I could think.
Do sit down and tell me, and please have a drink.'

The ghost in his phosphorous cloak gave a roar
And floated about between ceiling and floor.
He walked through a wall and returned through a pane
And back up the chimney and came down again.

Said the Colonel, 'With laughter I'm feeling quite
                           weak!'
(As trickles of merriment ran down his cheek).
My house-warming party I hope you won't spurn.
You *must* say you'll come and you'll give us a turn!'

At this, the poor spectre – quite out of his wits –
Proceeded to shake himself almost to bits.
He rattled his chains and he clattered his bones
And he filled the whole castle with mumbles and
                           moans.

But Colonel Fazackerley, just as before,
Was simply delighted and called out, 'Encore!'
At which the ghost vanished, his efforts in vain,
And never was seen at the castle again.

'Oh dear, what a pity!' said Colonel Fazack.
'I don't know his name, so I can't call him back.'
And then with a smile that was hard to define,
Colonel Fazackerley went in to dine.

ROALD DAHL

Extract from *The Witches:*
'Down Vith Children! Do Them In!'

'Down vith children! Do them in!
Boil their bones and fry their skin!
Bish them, sqvish them, bash them, mash
    them!
Brrreak them, shake them, slash them, smash
    them!
Offer chocs vith magic powder!
Say "Eat up!" then say it louder.
Crrram them full of sticky eats,
Send them home still guzzling sveets.
And in the morning little fools
Go marching off to separate schools.
A girl feels sick and goes all pale.
She yells, "Hey look! I've grrrown a tail!"
A boy who's standing next to her
Screams, "Help! I think I'm grrrowing fur!"
Another shouts, "Vee look like frrreaks!
There's viskers growing on our cheeks!"
A boy who vos extremely tall
Cries Out, "Vot's wrong? I'm grrrowing small!"
Four tiny legs begin to sprrrout
From everybody rrround about.
And all at vunce, all in a trrrice,
There are no children! Only MICE!

In every school is mice galore
All rrrunning rrround the school-rrroom floor!
And all the poor demented teachers
Is yelling, "Hey, who are these crrreatures?"
They stand upon the desks and shout,
"Get out, you filthy mice! Get out!
Vill someone fetch some mouse-trrraps,
      please!
And don't forrrget to bring the cheese!"
Now mouse-trrraps come and every trrrap
Goes *snippy-snip* and *snappy-snap*.
The mouse-trrraps have a powerful spring,
The springs go *crack* and *snap* and *ping*!
Is lovely noise for us to hear!
Is music to a vitch's ear!
Dead mice is every place arrround,
Piled two feet deep upon the grrround,
Vith teachers searching left and rrright,
But not a single child in sight!
The teachers cry, "Vot's going on?
Oh vhere have all the children gone?
Is half-past nine and as a rrrule
They're never late as this for school!"
Poor teachers don't know vot to do.
Some sit and rrread, and just a few
Amuse themselves throughout the day
By sveeping all the mice avay.
AND ALL US VITCHES SHOUT HOORAY!'

EVE MERRIAM

Catch a Little Rhyme

Once upon a time
I caught a little rhyme

I set it on the floor
but it ran right out the door

I chased it on my bicycle
but it melted to an icicle

I scooped it up in my hat
but it turned into a cat

I caught it by the tail
but it stretched into a whale

I followed it in a boat
but it changed into a goat

When I fed it tin and paper
it became a tall skyscraper

Then it grew into a kite
and flew far out of sight . . .

SYDNEY CARTER

Lord of the Dance

I danced in the morning
When the world was begun,
And I danced in the moon
And the stars and the sun
And I came down from heaven
And I danced on the earth –
At Bethlehem I had my birth.

Dance then wherever you may be;
I am the Lord of the Dance, said he,
I'll lead you all, wherever you may be,
I will lead you all in the Dance, said he.

I danced for the scribe
And the pharisee,
But they would not dance
And they couldn't follow me;
I danced for the fishermen,
For James and John –
They came with me
And the dance went on.

I danced on the Sabbath
And I cured the lame;
The holy people
Said it was a shame;
They whipped and they stripped
And they hung me high,
And they left me there
On a Cross to die.

I danced on a Friday
When the sky turned black –
It's hard to dance
With the devil on your back;
They buried my body
And they thought I'd gone –
But I am the dance
And I still go on.

They cut me down
And I leapt up high –
I am the life
That'll never, never die;
I'll live in you
If you'll live in me –
I am the Lord
Of the Dance, said he.

Dance then wherever you may be;
I am the Lord of the Dance, said he,
I'll lead you all, wherever you may be,
I will lead you all in the Dance, said he.

JUDITH WRIGHT

Magpies

Along the road the magpies walk
with hands in pockets, left and right.
They tilt their heads, and stroll and talk.
In their well-fitted black and white

they look like certain gentlemen
who seem most nonchalant and wise
until their meal is served – and then
what clashing beaks, what greedy eyes!

But not one man that I have heard
throws back his head in such a song
of grace and praise – no man nor bird.
Their greed is brief; their joy is long.
For each is born with such a throat
as thanks his God with every note.

Full Moon Rhyme

There's a hare in the moon tonight,
crouching alone in the bright
buttercup field of the moon;
and all the dogs in the world
howl at the hare in the moon.

'I chased that hare to the sky,'
the hungry dogs all cry.
'The hare jumped into the moon
and left me here in the cold.
I chased that hare to the moon.'

'Come down again, mad hare.
We can see you there,'
the dogs all howl to the moon.
'Come down again to the world,
you mad black hare in the moon,

or we will grow wings and fly
up to the star-grassed sky
to hunt you out of the moon,'
the hungry dogs of the world
howl at the hare in the moon.

DYLAN THOMAS

The Song of the Mischievous Dog

There are many who say that a dog has its day,
    And a cat has a number of lives;
There are others who think that a lobster is pink,
    And that bees never work in their hives.
There are fewer, of course, who insist that a horse
    Has a horn and two humps on its head,
And a fellow who jests that a mare can build nests
    Is as rare as a donkey that's red.
Yet in spite of all this, I have moments of bliss,
    For I cherish a passion for bones,
And though doubtful of biscuit, I'm willing to risk it,
    And I love to chase rabbits and stones.
But my greatest delight is to take a good bite
    At a calf that is plump and delicious;
And if I indulge in a bite at a bulge,
    Let's hope you won't think me too vicious.

LAURIE LEE

Apples

Behold the apples' rounded worlds:
juice-green of July rain,
the black polestar of flower, the rind
mapped with its crimson stain.

The russet, crab and cottage red
burn to the sun's hot brass,
then drop like sweat from every branch
and bubble in the grass.

They lie as wanton as they fall,
and where they fall and break,
the stallion clamps his crunching jaws,
the starling stabs his beak.

In each plump gourd the cidery bite
of boys' teeth tears the skin;
the waltzing wasp consumes his share,
the bent worm enters in.

I, with as easy hunger, take
entire my season's dole;
welcome the ripe, the sweet, the sour,
the hollow and the whole.

GEORGE BARKER

I Never See the Stars at Night

I never see the stars at night
    waltzing round the Moon
without wondering why they dance when
    no one plays a tune.

I hear no fiddles in the air
    or high and heavenly band
but round about they dance, the stars
    for ever hand in hand.

I think that wise ventriloquist
    the Old Man in the Moon
whistles so that only stars
    can hear his magic tune.

They Call to One Another

They call to one another
   in the prisons of the sea
the mermen and mermaidens
   bound under lock and key
down in the green and salty dens
   and dungeons of the sea,
lying about in chains but
   dying to be free:
and this is why shortsighted men
   believe them not to be
for down to their dark dungeons it
   is very hard to see.

But sometimes morning fishermen
   drag up in the net
bits of bright glass or the silver comb
   of an old vanity set
or a letter rather hard to read
   because it is still wet
sent to remind us never, never
   never to forget
the mermen and mermaidens
   in the prisons of the sea
who call to one another
   when the stars of morning rise
and the stars of evening set
   for I have heard them calling
and I can hear them, yet.

Elephant

Elephants are elephants
the way mountains are mountains
the way palaces are palaces
and railway trains railway trains.
There is absolutely
no point whatever
in denying that Elephants
are extremely clever.
When an Elephant retreats
he places his foot
backwards where it
was formerly put
because a retreating
Elephant knows
he was safe when he came
so he's safe when he goes.
The Elephant dances
more lightly than
any other mastodon
can can-can.
Indeed the tremendous
Elephant
does everything
other animals can't
such as turn his nose
into a hose
or – (no magician's
a cleverer fellah!) –

his ear into
an umbrella.
He's a house on the ground
that can stroll about,
he's an island in water
when his back sticks out,
he's stronger than towers
built of bricks and mortar,
he can carry a trunk
like a railway porter,
he's the Lord of Peace
and the Lord of Slaughter,
and he's gentle as
a Ranee's daughter
and if you don't love him,
well, you oughta.

EDWARD LOWBURY

The Huntsman

Kagwa hunted the lion,
  Through bush and forest went his spear.
One day he found the skull of a man
  And said to it, 'How did you come here?'
The skull opened its mouth and said,
  'Talking brought me here.'

Kagwa hurried home;
  Went to the king's chair and spoke:
'In the forest I found a talking skull.'
  The king was silent. Then he said slowly,
'Never since I was born of my mother
  Have I seen or heard of a skull which spoke.'

The king called out to his guards:
  'Two of you now go with him
And find this talking skull;
  But if his tale is a lie
And the skull speaks no word,
  This Kagwa himself must die.'

They rode into the forest;
　For days and nights they found nothing.
At last they saw the skull; Kagwa
　Said to it, 'How did you come here?'
The skull said nothing. Kagwa implored,
　But the skull said nothing.

The guards said, 'Kneel down.'
　They killed him with sword and spear.
Then the skull opened its mouth;
　'Huntsman, how did you come here?'
And the dead man answered,
　'Talking brought me here.'

IAN SERRAILLIER

The Crooked Man

There was a crooked man was once a little lad,
He hadn't any mother and he hadn't any dad,
He hadn't any home or a family tree.
Where did he come from? Don't ask me.

This little crooked lad grew up to be a man
(One leg stopped where the other one began).
He hobbled with a stick for a whole crooked mile
And found a crooked sixpence upon a crooked stile.

He ran to a shop then – a-tinkle went the bell.
'Good morning to you, missus, and what do you sell?'
'I've candy and a barrow and a black silk hat.'
'None of those, thank you, I'll buy a crooked cat.'

He bought a crooked cat and it caught a crooked mouse
Pitter-patter down the gutter of an old farm-house.
'Be friends with me, mousie, there's no harm meant,
For we're all of us crooked here but me, and I'm bent.'

They jogged along together but they couldn't keep in
step.
'Right turn!' said the crooked man – they turned to the
left.
But he brought them at last to a little crooked house,
And he lived there for ever with the pussy and the mouse.

There was a crooked man and he walked a crooked mile,
He found a crooked sixpence upon a crooked stile.
He bought a crooked cat and it caught a crooked mouse,
And they all lived together in a little crooked house.

The Visitor

A crumbling churchyard, the sea and the moon;
The waves had gouged out grave and bone;
A man was walking, late and alone . . .

He saw a skeleton on the ground;
A ring on a bony finger he found.

He ran home to his wife and gave her the ring.
'Oh, where did you get?' He said not a thing.

'It's the loveliest ring in the world,' she said,
As it glowed on her finger. They slipped off to bed.

At midnight they woke. In the dark outside,
'Give me my ring!' a chill voice cried.

'What was that, William? What did it say?'
'Don't worry, my dear. It'll soon go away.'

'I'm coming!' A skeleton opened the door.
'Give me my ring!' It was crossing the floor.

'What was that, William? What did it say?'
'Don't worry, my dear. It'll soon go away.'

'I'm reaching you now! I'm climbing the bed.'
The wife pulled the sheet right over her head.

It was torn from her grasp and tossed in the air:
'I'll drag you out of bed by the hair!'

'What was that, William? What did it say?'
'Throw the ring through the window! THROW IT
                                        AWAY!'

She threw it. The skeleton leapt from the sill,
Scooped up the ring and clattered downhill,
Fainter . . . and fainter . . . Then all was still.

KENNETH PATCHEN

The Magical Mouse

I am the magical mouse
I don't eat cheese
I eat sunsets
And the tops of trees

I don't wear fur

I wear funnels
Of lost ships and the weather
That's under dead leaves
I am the magical mouse

I don't fear cats

Or woodsowls
I do as I please
Always
I don't eat crusts
I am the magical mouse
I eat
Little birds and maidens

That taste like dust.

MERVYN PEAKE

The Trouble with Geraniums

The trouble with geraniums
is that they're much too red!
The trouble with my toast is that
it's far too full of bread.

The trouble with a diamond
is that's it's much too bright.
The same applies to fish and stars
and the electric light.

The trouble with the stars I see
lies in the way they fly.
The trouble with myself is all
self-centred in the eye.

The trouble with my looking-glass
is that it shows me, me:
there's trouble in all sorts of things
where it should never be.

Aunts and Uncles

When Aunty Jane
Became a Crane
She put one leg behind her head;
And even when the clock struck ten
Refused to go to bed.

When Aunty Grace
Became a Plaice
She all but vanished sideways on;
Except her nose
And pointed toes
The rest of her was gone.

When Uncle Grog
Became a Dog
He hid himself for shame;
He sometimes hid his bone as well
And wouldn't hear the front-door bell,
Or answer to his name.

When Aunty Flo
Became a Crow
She had a bed put in a tree;
And there she lay
And read all day
Of ornithology.

When Aunty Vi
Became a Fly
Her favourite nephew
Sought her life;
How could he know
That with each blow
He bruised his Uncle's wife?

When Uncle Sam
Became a Ham
We did not care to carve him up;
He struggled so;
We let him go
And gave him to the pup.

When Aunty Nag
Became a Crag
She stared across the dawn,
To where her spouse
Kept open house
With ladies on the lawn.

When Aunty Mig
Became a Pig
She floated on the briny breeze,
With irritation in her heart
And warts upon her knees.

When Aunty Jill
Became a Pill
She stared all day through dark-blue glass;
And always sneered
When men appeared
To ask her how she was.

When Uncle Jake
Became a Snake
He never found it out;
And so as no one mentions it
One sees him still about.

Little Spider

Little spider
spiding sadly
in the webly
light of leaves!
Why deride a
spide's mentadly
when its hebly
full of grieves?

Little spider
legged and lonely
in the bony
way of thieves.
Where's the fly-da
on the phonebly?

O'er Seas That Have No Beaches

O'er seas that have no beaches
To end their waves upon,
I floated with twelve peaches,
A sofa and a swan.

The blunt waves crashed above us
The sharp waves burst around,
There was no one to love us,
No hope of being found –

Where, on the notched horizon
So endlessly a-drip,
I saw all of a sudden
No sign of any ship.

O Here It Is! And There It Is!

O here it is! And there it is!
And no one knows whose share it is
Nor dares to stake a claim –
But we have seen it in the air
A fairy like a William Pear –
With but itself to blame.

A thug it is – and smug it is
And like a floating pug it is
Above the orchard trees
It has no right – no right at all
To soar above the orchard wall
With chilblains on its knees.

JOHN WALSH

The Bully Asleep

One afternoon, when grassy
Scents through the classroom crept,
Bill Craddock laid his head
Down on his desk, and slept.

The children came round him:
Jimmy, Roger, and Jane;
They lifted his head timidly
And let it sink again.

'Look, he's gone sound asleep, Miss,'
Said Jimmy Adair;
'He stays up all the night, you see;
His mother doesn't care.'

'Stand away from him, children.'
Miss Andrews stooped to see.
'Yes, he's asleep; go on
With your writing, and let him be.'

'Now's a good chance!' whispered Jimmy;
And he snatched Bill's pen and hid it.
'Kick him under the desk, hard;
He won't know who did it.'

'Fill all his pockets with rubbish –
Paper, apple-cores, chalk.'
So they plotted, while Jane
Sat wide-eyed at their talk.

Not caring, not hearing,
Bill Craddock he slept on;
Lips parted, eyes closed –
Their cruelty gone.

'Stick him with pins!' muttered Roger.
'Ink down his neck!' said Jim.
But Jane, tearful and foolish,
Wanted to comfort him.

NORMAN MacCAIG

Frogs

Frogs sit more solid
than anything sits. In mid-leap they are
parachutists falling
in a free fall. They die on roads
with arms across their chests and
heads high.

I love frogs that sit
like Buddha, that fall without
parachutes, that die
like Italian tenors.

Above all, I love them because,
pursued in water, they never
panic so much that they fail
to make stylish triangles
with their ballet dancer's
legs.

Blind Horse

He snuffles towards
pouches of water in the grass
and doesn't drink
when he finds them.

He twitches listlessly
at sappy grass stems and stands
stone still, his hanging head
caricatured with a scribble
of green whiskers.

Sometimes that head swings high,
ears cock – and he stares
down a long sound,
he stares and whinnies
for what never comes.

His eyes never close,
not in the heat of the day
when his leather lip droops and
he wears blinkers of flies.

At any time of the night
you hear him in his dark field
stamp the ground, stamp
the world down, waiting impatiently
for the light to break.

MARGARET WISE BROWN

The Secret Song

Who saw the petals
  drop from the rose?
I, said the spider,
But nobody knows.

Who saw the sunset
  flash on a bird?
I, said the fish,
But nobody heard.

Who saw the fog
  come over the sea?
I, said the sea pigeon,
Only me.

Who saw the first
  green light of the sun?
I, said the night owl,
The only one.

Who saw the moss
  creep over the stone?
I, said the gray fox,
All alone.

PHOEBE HESKETH

Truant

Sing a song of sunlight
My pocket's full of sky —
Starling's egg for April
Jay's feather for July.
And here's a thorn bush three bags full
Of drift-white wool.

They call him dunce, and yet he can discern
Each mouse-brown bird,
And call its name and whistle back its call,
And spy among the fern
Delicate movement of a furred
Fugitive creature hiding from the day.
Discovered secrets magnify his play
Into a vocation.

Laughing at education
He knows where the redshank hides her nest, perceives
a reed-patch tremble when a coot lays seige
To water territory.
Nothing escapes his eye:
A ladybird
Slides like a blood-drop down a spear of grass;
The sapphire sparkle of a dragon-fly
Redeems a waste of weeds.
Collecting acorns, telling the beads of the year
On yew tree berries, his mind's too full for speech.

Back in the classroom he can never find
Answers to dusty questions, yet could teach,

    Deeper than knowledge,
    Geometry of twigs
    Scratched on a sunlit wall;
    History in stones,
    Seasons told by the fields' calendar –
    Living languages of Spring and Fall.

JAMES REEVES

Spells

I dance and dance without any feet –
This is the spell of the ripening wheat.

With never a tongue I've a tale to tell –
This is the meadow-grasses' spell.

I give you health without any fee –
This is the spell of the apple-tree.

I rhyme and riddle without any book –
This is the spell of the bubbling brook.

Without any legs I run for ever –
This is the spell of the mighty river.

I fall for ever and not at all –
This is the spell of the waterfall.

Without a voice I roar aloud –
This is the spell of the thunder-cloud.

No button or seam has my white coat –
This is the spell of the leaping goat.

I can cheat strangers with never a word –
This is the spell of the cuckoo-bird.

We have tongues in plenty but speak no names –
This is the spell of the fiery flames.

The creaking door has a spell to riddle –
I play a tune without any fiddle.

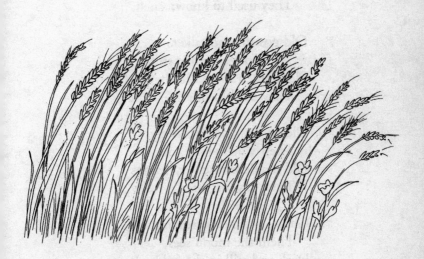

Trees in the Moonlight

Trees in the moonlight stand
  Still as a steeple,
And so quiet they seem like ghosts
  Of country people –

Dead farmers and their wives
  Of long, long ago,
Haunting the countryside
  They used to know;

Old gossips and talkers
  With tongues gone still;
Ploughmen rooted in the land
  They used to till;

Old carters and harvesters,
  Their wheels long rotten;
Old maids whose very names
  Time has forgotten.

Ghosts are they hereabouts;
  Them the moon sees,
Dark and still in the fields
  Like sleeping trees.

Long nights in autumn
  Hear them strain and cry,
Torn with a wordless sorrow
  As the gale sweeps by.

Spring makes fresh buds appear
  On the old boughs,
As if it could to their old wishes
  These ghosts arouse.

Trees in the summer night
  By moonlight linger on
So quiet they seem like ghosts
  Of people gone,

And it would be small wonder
  If at break of day
They heard the far-off cock-crow
  And fled away.

Rabbit and Lark

'Under the ground
    It's rumbly and dark
And interesting,'
    Said Rabbit to Lark.

Said Lark to Rabbit,
    'Up in the sky
There's plenty of room
    And it's airy and high.'

'Under the ground
    It's warm and dry.
Won't you live with me?'
    Was Rabbit's reply.

'The air's so sunny.
    I wish you'd agree,'
Said the little Lark,
    'To live with me.

But under the ground
    And up in the sky,
Larks can't burrow
    Nor rabbits fly.

So Skylark over
   And Rabbit under
They had to settle
   To live asunder.

And often these two friends
   Meet with a will
For a chat together
   On top of the hill.

W

The King sent for his wise men all
    To find a rhyme for W.
When they had thought a good long time
But could not think of a single rhyme,
    'I'm sorry,' said he, 'to trouble you.'

The Intruder

Two-boots in the forest walks,
Pushing through the bracken stalks.

Vanishing like a puff of smoke,
Nimbletails flies up the oak.

Longears helter-skelter shoots
Into his house among the roots.

At work upon the highest bark,
Tapperbill knocks off to hark.

Painted-wings through sun and shade
Flounces off along the glade.

Not a creature lingers by,
When clumping Two-boots comes to pry.

THEODORE ROETHKE

The Sloth

In moving-slow he has no Peer.
You ask him something in his Ear,
He thinks about it for a Year;

And, then, before he says a Word
There, upside down (unlike a Bird),
He will assume that you have Heard –

A most Ex-as-per-at-ing Lug.
But should you call his manner Smug,
He'll sigh and give his Branch a Hug;

Then off again to Sleep he goes,
Still swaying gently by his Toes,
And you just *know* he knows he knows.

The Serpent

There was a Serpent who had to sing.
There was. There was.
He simply gave up Serpenting.
Because. Because.

He didn't like his Kind of Life;
He couldn't find a proper Wife;
He was a Serpent with a soul;
He got no Pleasure down his Hole.
And so, of course, he had to Sing,
And Sing he did, like Anything!
The Birds, they were, they were Astounded;
And various Measures Propounded
To stop the Serpent's Awful Racket:
They bought a Drum. He wouldn't Whack it.
They sent, you always send, to Cuba
And got a Most Commodious Tuba;
They got a Horn, they got a Flute,
But Nothing would suit.
He said, 'Look, Birds, all this is futile:
I do *not* like to Bang or Tootle.'
And then he cut loose with a Horrible Note
That practically split the Top of his Throat.
'You see,' he said, with a Serpent's Leer,
'I'm Serious about my Singing Career!'
And the Woods Resounded with many a Shriek
As the Birds flew off to the End of Next Week.

My Papa's Waltz

The whisky on your breath
Could make a small boy dizzy;
But I hung on like death:
Such waltzing was not easy.

We romped until the pans
Slid from the kitchen shelf;
My mother's countenance
Could not unfrown itself.

The hand that held my wrist
Was battered on one knuckle;
At every step you missed
My right ear scraped a buckle.

You beat time on my head
With a palm caked hard by dirt,
Then waltzed me off to bed
Still clinging to your shirt.

KATHLEEN RAINE

Spell of Creation

Within the flower there lies a seed,
In the seed there springs a tree,
In the tree there spreads a wood.

In the wood there burns a fire,
And in the fire there melts a stone,
Within the stone a ring of iron.

Within the ring there lies an O,
In the O there looks an eye,
In the eye there swims a sea,

And in the sea reflected sky,
And in the sky there shines the sun,
In the sun a bird of gold.

In the bird there beats a heart,
And from the heart there flows a song,
And in the song there sings a word.

In the word there speaks a world,
A word of joy, a world of grief,
From joy and grief there springs my love.

Oh love, my love, there springs a world,
And on the world there shines a sun,
And in the sun there burns a fire.

In the fire consumes my heart,
And in my heart there beats a bird,
And in the bird there wakes an eye,

Within the eye, earth, sea and sky,
Earth, sky and sea within an O,
Lie like the seeds within the flower.

W. H. AUDEN

Night Mail
(Commentary for a G.P.O. Film)

I

This is the Night Mail crossing the Border,
Bringing the cheque and the postal order,

Letters for the rich, letters for the poor,
The shop at the corner, the girl next door.

Pulling up Beattock, a steady climb:
The gradient's against her, but she's on time.

Past cotton-grass and moorland boulder,
Shovelling white steam over her shoulder,

Snorting noisily, she passes
Silent miles of wind-bent grasses.

Birds turn their heads as she approaches,
Stare from bushes at her blank-faced coaches.

Sheep-dogs cannot turn her course;
They slumber on with paws across.

In the farm she passes no one wakes,
But a jug in a bedroom gently shakes.

II

Dawn freshens. Her climb is done.
Down towards Glasgow she descends,
Towards the steam tugs yelping down a glade of cranes
Towards the fields of apparatus, the furnaces
Set on the dark plain like gigantic chessmen.
All Scotland waits for her:
In dark glens, beside pale-green lochs,
Men long for news.

III

Letters of thanks, letters from banks,
Letters of joy from girl and boy,
Receipted bills and invitations
To inspect new stock or to visit relations,
And applications for situations,
And timid lovers' declarations,
And gossip, gossip from all the nations,

News circumstantial, news financial,
Letters with holiday snaps to enlarge in,
Letters with faces scrawled on the margin,
Letters from uncles, cousins and aunts,
Letters to Scotland from the South of France,
Letters of condolence to Highlands and Lowlands,
Written on paper of every hue,
    The pink, the violet, the white and the blue,
The chatty, the catty, the boring, the adoring,
The cold and official and the heart's outpouring,
Clever, stupid, short and long,
The typed and the printed and the spelt all wrong.

IV

Thousands are still asleep,
Dreaming of terrifying monsters
Or a friendly tea beside the band in Cranston's or
                                              Crawford's:
Asleep in working Glasgow, asleep in well-set Edinburgh,
Asleep in granite Aberdeen,
They continue their dreams,
But shall wake soon and hope for letters,
And none will hear the postman's knock
Without a quickening of the heart.
For who can bear to feel himself forgotten?

LYDIA PENDER

The Lizard

Still is your delicate head,
Like the head of an arrow;
Still is your delicate throat,
Rounded and narrow;
Still is your delicate back,
Patterned in silver and black,
And bright with the burnished sheen that the gum-tips
                                              share;
Even your delicate feet
Are still, still as the heat,
With a stillness alive and awake, and intensely aware.
Why do I catch my breath,
Held by your spell?
Listening, waiting – for what?
Will you not tell?
More alive in your quiet than ever the locust can be,
Shrilling his clamorous song from the shimmering tree;
More alive in your motionless grace, as the slow
                                              minutes die,
Than the scurrying ants that go hurrying busily by.
I know, if my shadow but fall by your feet on the stone,
In the wink of an eye,
Let me try –
Ah!
He's gone!

Giants

How would *you* like it –
Supposing that *you* were a snail,
And your eyes grew out on threads,
Gentle, and small, and frail –
If an enormous creature,
Reaching almost up to the distant skies,
Leaned down, and with his great finger touched your
eyes
Just for the fun
Of seeing you snatch them suddenly in
And cower, quivering, back
Into your pitiful shell, so brittle and thin?
Would you think it was fun then?
Would you think it was fun?

And how would *you* like it,
Supposing you were a frog,
An emerald scrap with a pale, trembling throat
In a cool and shadowed bog,
If a tremendous monster,
Tall, tall, so that his head seemed lost in mist,
Leaned over, and clutched you up in his great fist
Just for the joy
Of watching you jump, scramble, tumble, fall,
In graceless, shivering dread,
Back into the trampled reeds that were grown so tall?
Would you think it a joy then?
Would you think it a joy?

SIR JOHN BETJEMAN

Diary of a Church Mouse
(Lines, written to order on a set subject, to
be spoken on the wireless.)

Here among long-discarded cassocks,
Damp stools, and half-split open hassocks,
Here where the Vicar never looks
I nibble through old service books.
Lean and alone I spend my days
Behind this Church of England baize.
I share my dark forgotten room
With two oil-lamps and half a broom.
The cleaner never bothers me,
So here I eat my frugal tea.
My bread is sawdust mixed with straw;
My jam is polish for the floor.
   Christmas and Easter may be feasts
For congregations and for priests,
And so may Whitsun. All the same,
They do not fill my meagre frame.
For me the only feast at all
Is Autumn's Harvest Festival,
When I can satisfy my want
With ears of corn around the font.
I climb the eagle's brazen head
To burrow through a loaf of bread.
I scramble up the pulpit stair

And gnaw the marrows hanging there.
   It is enjoyable to taste
These items ere they go to waste,
But how annoying when one finds
That other mice with pagan minds
Come into church my food to share
Who have no proper business there.
Two field mice who have no desire
To be baptized, invade the choir.
A large and most unfriendly rat
Comes in to see what we are at.
He says he thinks there is no God
And yet he comes . . . it's rather odd.
This year he stole a sheaf of wheat
(It screened our special preacher's seat),
And prosperous mice from fields away
Come in to hear the organ play,
And under cover of its notes
Ate through the altar's sheaf of oats.
A Low Church mouse, who thinks that I
Am too papistical, and High,
Yet somehow doesn't think it wrong
To munch through Harvest Evensong,
While I, who starve the whole year through,
Must share my food with rodents who
Except at this time of the year
Not once inside the church appear.
   Within the human world I know
Such goings-on could not be so,
For human beings only do
What their religion tells them to.
They read the Bible every day

And always, night and morning, pray,
And just like me, the good church mouse,
Worship each week in God's own house.
  But all the same it's strange to me
How very full the church can be
With people I don't see at all
Except at Harvest Festival.

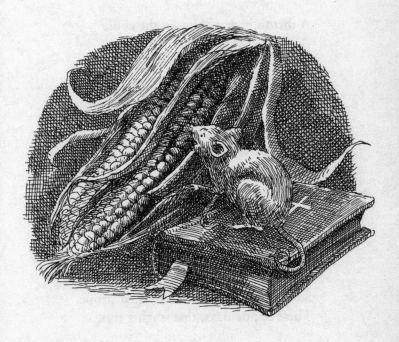

LEONARD CLARK

The Singing Time

Plumtrees in orchards day and night
Make all the world a dream of white.

A thrush is throbbing in the copse
A jewelled song that never stops.

Bluebells in drifts of deep sapphire
Have set the ferny woods on fire.

A cuckoo calls his tune until
First shadows fall on field and hill.

Tulips in solid squads and teams
Are almost bursting at the seams.

A jenny wren with needle eyes
Is in the bushes catching flies.

So flowers and birds are in their prime,
These happy days, this singing time.

Earth-Worm

Do
you
squirm
when
you
see
an earth-worm?
I never
do squirm
because I think
a big fat worm
is really rather clever
the way it can shrink
and go
so small
without
a sound
into the ground.
And then
what about
all
that
work it does
and no oxygen
or miner's hat?
Marvellous
you have to admit,
even if you don't like fat
pink worms a bit,

how with that
thin
slippery skin
it makes its way
day after day
through the soil,
such honest toil.
And don't forget
the dirt
it eats, I bet
you wouldn't like to come out
at night to squirt
it all over the place
with no eyes in your face:
I doubt
too if you know
an earth-worm is deaf, but
it can hear YOU go
to and fro
even if you cut
it in half.
Do not laugh
or squirm
again
when
you
suddenly
see
a worm.

Good Company

I sleep in a room at the top of the house
With a flea, and a fly, and a soft-scratching mouse,
And a spider that hangs by a thread from the ceiling,
Who gives me each day such a curious feeling
When I watch him at work on the beautiful weave
Of his web that's so fine I can hardly believe
It won't all end up in such terrible tangles,
For he sways as he weaves, and spins as he dangles.
I cannot get up to that spider, I know,
And I hope he won't get down to me here below,
And yet when I wake in the chill morning air
I'd miss him if he were not still swinging there,
For I have in my room such good company,
There's him, and the mouse, and the fly, and the flea.

A. L. ROWSE

The White Cat of Trenarren
(for Beryl Cloke)

He was a mighty hunter in his youth
At Polmear all day on the mound, on the pounce
For anything moving, rabbit or bird or mouse –
　My cat and I grow old together.

After a day's hunting he'd come into the house
Delicate ears stuck all with fleas.
At Trenarren I've heard him sigh with pleasure
After a summer's day in the long-grown leas –
　My cat and I grow old together.

When I was a child I played all day,
With only a little cat for companion,
At solitary games of my own invention
Under the table or up in the green bay –
　My cat and I grow old together.

When I was a boy I wandered the roads
Up to the downs by gaunt Carn Grey,
Wrapt in a dream at end of day,
All round me the moor, below me the bay –
　My cat and I grow old together.

Now we are too often apart, yet
Turning out of Central Park into the Plaza,
Or walking Michigan Avenue against the lake-wind,
I see a little white shade in the shrubbery
Of far-off Trenarren, never far from my mind –
  My cat and I grow old together.

When I come home from too much travelling,
Cautiously he comes out of his lair to my call,
Receives me at first with a shy reproach
At long absence to him incomprehensible –
  My cat and I grow old together.

Incapable of much or long resentment,
He scratches at my door to be let out
In early morning in the ash moonlight,
Or red dawn breaking through Mother Bond's
                                    spinney –
  My cat and I grow old together.

No more frisking as of old,
Or chasing his shadow over the lawn,
But a dignified old person, tickling
His nose against twig or flower in the border,
Until evening falls and bed-time's in order,
Unable to keep eyes open any longer
He waits for me to carry him upstairs
To nestle all night snug at foot of bed –
  My cat and I grow old together.

Careful of his licked and polished appearance,
Ears like shell-whorls pink and transparent,
White plume waving proudly over the paths,
Against a background of sea and blue hydrangeas –
  My cat and I grow old together.

STEVIE SMITH

The Frog Prince

I am a frog
I live under a spell
I live at the bottom
Of a green well.

And here I must wait
Until a maiden places me
On her royal pillow
And kisses me
In her father's palace.

The story is familiar
Everybody knows it well
But do other enchanted people feel as nervous
As I do? The stories do not tell.

Ask if they will be happier
When the changes come
As already they are fairly happy
In a frog's doom?

I have been a frog now
For a hundred years
And in all this time
I have not shed many tears,

I am happy, I like the life,
Can swim for many a mile
(When I have hopped to the river)
And am for ever agile.

And the quietness,
Yes, I like to be quiet
I am habituated
To a quiet life.

But always when I think these thoughts
As I sit in my well
Another thought comes to me and says:
It is part of the spell

To be happy
To work up contentment
To make much of being a frog
To fear disenchantment

Says, It will be *heavenly*
To be set free,
Cries, *Heavenly* the girl who disenchants
And the royal times, *heavenly*,
And I think it will be.

Come, then, royal girl and royal times,
Come quickly,
I can be happy until you come
But I cannot be heavenly,
Only disenchanted people
Can be heavenly.

The Old Sweet Dove of Wiveton

'Twas the voice of the sweet dove
I heard him move,
I heard him cry:
Love, love.

High in the chestnut tree
Is the nest of the old dove
And there he sits solitary
Crying, Love, love.

The gray of this heavy day
Makes the green of the tree's leaves and the grass
                                        brighter,
And the flowers of the chestnut tree whiter,
And whiter the flowers of the high cow-parsley.

So still is the air,
So heavy the sky,
You can hear the splash
Of the water falling from the green grass
As Red and Honey push by,
The old dogs,
Gone away, gone hunting by the marsh bogs.
Happy the retriever dogs in their pursuit,
Happy in bog-mud the busy foot.

Now all is silent, it is silent again,
In the sombre day and the beginning soft rain,
It is a silence made more actual
By the moan from the high tree that is occasional.

Where in his nest above
Still sits the old dove,
Murmuring solitary,
Crying for pain,
Crying most melancholy
Again and again.

OGDEN NASH

The Wombat

The wombat lives across the seas,
Among the fair Antipodes.
He may exist on nuts and berries,
Or then again, on missionaries;
His distant habit precludes
Conclusive knowledge of his moods.
But I would not engage the wombat
In any form of mortal combat.

The Purist

I give you now Professor Twist,
A conscientious scientist.
Trustees exclaimed, 'He never bungles!'
And sent him off to distant jungles.
Camped on a tropic riverside,
One day he missed his living bride.
She had, the guide informed him later,
Been eaten by an alligator.
Professor Twist could not but smile.
'You mean,' he said, 'a crocodile.'

The Parent

Children aren't happy with nothing to ignore,
And that's what parents were created for.

Adventures of Isabel

Isabel met an enormous bear,
Isabel, Isabel, didn't care;
The bear was hungry, the bear was ravenous,
The bear's big mouth was cruel and cavernous.
The bear said, Isabel, glad to meet you,
How do, Isabel, now I'll eat you!
Isabel, Isabel, didn't worry,
Isabel didn't scream or scurry.
She washed her hands and she straightened her hair up,
Then Isabel quietly ate the bear up.

Once in a night as black as pitch
Isabel met a wicked old witch.
The witch's face was cross and wrinkled,
The witch's gums with teeth were sprinkled.
Ho ho, Isabel! the old witch crowed,
I'll turn you into an ugly toad!
Isabel, Isabel, didn't worry,
Isabel didn't scream or scurry.
She showed no rage and she showed no rancor,
But she turned the witch into milk and drank her.

Isabel met a hideous giant,
Isabel continued self reliant.
The giant was hairy, the giant was horrid,
He had one eye in the middle of his forehead.
Good morning, Isabel, the giant said,
I'll grind your bones to make my bread.
Isabel, Isabel, didn't worry,
Isabel didn't scream or scurry.
She nibbled the zwieback that she always fed off
And when it was gone, she cut the giant's head off.

Isabel met a troublesome doctor,
He punched and he poked till he really shocked her.
The doctor's talk was of coughs and chills
And the doctor's satchel bulged with pills.
The doctor said unto Isabel,
Swallow this, it will make you well.
Isabel, Isabel, didn't worry,
Isabel didn't scream or scurry.
She took those pills from the pill concocter,
And Isabel calmly cured the doctor.

DAVID McCORD

Glowworm

Never talk down to a glowworm –
Such as *What do you knowworm?*
How's it down belowworm?
Guess you're quite a slowworm.
No. Just say
　　　　　Helloworm!

Pad and Pencil

I drew a rabbit. John erased him
and not the dog I said had chased him.

I drew a bear on another page,
but John said, 'Put him in a cage.'

I drew some mice. John drew the cat
with nasty claws. The mice saw that.

I got them off the page real fast:
the things I draw don't *ever* last.

We drew a bird with one big wing:
he couldn't fly worth anything,

but sat there crumpled on a limb.
John's pencil did a job on *him*.

Three bats were next. I made them fly.
John smudged one out against the sky

above an owl he said could hoot.
He helped me with my wolf. The brute

had lots too long a tail, but we
concealed it all behind a tree.

By then I couldn't think of much
except to draw a rabbit hutch;

but since we had no rabbit now
I drew what must have been a cow,

with curvy horns stuck through the slats –
they both looked something like the bats.

And feeling sad about the bear
inside his cage, I saw just where

I'd draw the door to let him out.
And that's just all of it, about.

ROBERT GRAVES

The Alice Jean

One moonlight night a ship drove in,
  A ghost ship from the west,
Drifting with bare mast and lone tiller;
  Like a mermaid drest
In long green weed and barnacles
  She beached and came to rest.

All the watchers of the coast
  Flocked to view the sight;
Men and women, streaming down
  Through the summer night,
Found her standing tall and ragged
  Beached in the moonlight.

Then one old woman stared aghast:
  'The *Alice Jean*? But no!
The ship that took my Ned from me
  Sixty years ago –
Drifted back from the utmost west
  With the ocean's flow?

'Caught and caged in the weedy pool
  Beyond the western brink,
Where crewless vessels lie and rot
  In waters black as ink,

Torn out at last by a sudden gale –
    Is it the *Jean*, you think?'

A hundred women gaped at her,
    The menfolk nudged and laughed,
But none could find a likelier story
    For the strange craft
With fear and death and desolation
    Rigged fore and aft.

The blind ship came forgotten home
    To all but one of these,
Of whom none dared to climb aboard her:
    And by and by the breeze
Veered hard about, and the *Alice Jean*
    Foundered in foaming seas.

The Six Badgers

As I was a-hoeing, a-hoeing my lands,
Six badgers walked up, with white wands in their hands.
They formed a ring round me and, bowing, they said:
'Hurry home, Farmer George, for the table is spread!
There's pie in the oven, there's beef on the plate:
Hurry home, Farmer George, if you would not be late!'

So homeward went I, but could not understand
Why six fine dog-badgers with white wands in hand
Should seek me out hoeing, and bow in a ring,
And all to inform me so common a thing!

The Penny Fiddle

Yesterday I bought a penny fiddle
   And put it to my chin to play,
But I found that the strings were painted,
   So I threw my fiddle away.

A gipsy girl found my penny fiddle
   As it lay abandoned there;
When she asked me if she might keep it,
   I told her I did not care.

Then she drew such music from the fiddle
   With help of a farthing bow,
That I offered five shillings for the secret.
   But, alas, she would not let it go.

Welsh Incident

'But that was nothing to what things came out
From the sea-caves of Criccieth yonder.'
'What were they? Mermaids? dragons? ghosts?'
'Nothing at all of any things like that.'
'What were they, then?'
                        'All sorts of queer things,
Things never seen or heard or written about,
Very strange, un-Welsh, utterly peculiar
Things. Oh, solid enough they seemed to touch,
Had anyone dared it. Marvellous creation,
All various shapes and sizes, and no sizes,
All new, each perfectly unlike his neighbour,
Though all came moving slowly out together.'
'Describe just one of them.'
                        'I am unable.'
'What were their colours?'
                        'Mostly nameless colours,
Colours you'd like to see; but one was puce
Or perhaps more crimson, but not purplish.
Some had no colour.'
                        'Tell me, had they legs?'
'Not a leg nor foot among them that I saw.'
'But did these things come out in any order?
What o'clock was it? What was the day of the week?
Who else was present? How was the weather?'
'I was coming to that. It was half-past three
On Easter Tuesday last. The sun was shining.

The Harlech Silver Band played *Marchog Jesu*
On thirty-seven shimmering instruments,
Collecting for Caernarvon's (Fever) Hospital Fund.
The populations of Pwllheli, Criccieth,
Portmadoc, Borth, Tremadoc, Penrhyndeudraeth,
Were all assembled. Criccieth's mayor addressed them
First in good Welsh and then in fluent English,
Twisting his fingers in his chain of office,
Welcoming the things. They came out on the sand,
Not keeping time to the band, moving seaward
Silently at a snail's pace. But at last
The most odd, indescribable thing of all,
Which hardly one man there could see for wonder,
Did something recognizably a something.'
'Well, what?'
                  'It made a noise.'
                                    'A frightening noise?'
'No, no.'
          'A musical noise? A noise of scuffling?'
'No, but a very loud, respectable noise –
Like groaning to oneself on Sunday morning
In Chapel, close before the second psalm.'
'What did the mayor do?'
                        'I was coming to that.'

RACHEL FIELD

Something Told the Wild Geese

Something told the wild geese
   It was time to go.
Though the field lay golden
   Something whispered, 'Snow.'
Leaves were green and stirring,
   Berries, lustre-glossed,
But beneath warm feathers
   Something cautioned, 'Frost.'
All the sagging orchards
   Steamed with amber spice,
But each wild breast stiffened
   At remembered ice.
Something told the wild geese
   It was time to fly –
Summer sun was on their wings,
   Winter in their cry.

E. E. CUMMINGS

little tree

little tree
little silent Christmas tree
you are so little
you are more like a flower

who found you in the green forest
and were you very sorry to come away?
see i will comfort you
because you smell so sweetly

i will kiss your cool bark
and hug you safe and tight
just as your mother would,
only don't be afraid

look the spangles
that sleep all the year in a dark box
dreaming of being taken out and allowed to shine,
the balls the chains red and gold the fluffy threads,

put up your little arms
and i'll give them all to you to hold
every finger shall have its ring
and there won't be a single place dark or unhappy

when you're quite dressed
you'll stand in the window for everyone to see
and how they'll stare!
oh but you'll be very proud

and my little sister and i will take hands
and looking up at our beautiful tree
we'll dance and sing
'Noel Noel'

maggie and milly and molly and may

maggie and milly and molly and may
went down to the beach (to play one day)

and maggie discovered a shell that sang
so sweetly she couldn't remember her troubles, and

milly befriended a stranded star
whose rays five languid fingers were;

and molly was chased by a horrible thing
which raced sideways while blowing bubbles: and

may came home with a smooth round stone
as small as a world and as large as alone.

For whatever we lose (like a you or a me)
it's always ourselves we find in the sea

in Just-

in Just-
spring   when the world is mud-
luscious the little
lame balloonman

whistles   far   and wee

 and eddieandbill come
running from marbles and
piracies and it's
spring

 when the world is puddle-wonderful

 the queer
old balloonman whistles
far   and   wee
and bettyandisbel come dancing

 from hop-scotch and jump-rope and

it's
spring
and
          the
                    goat-footed

 balloonMan   whistles
far
and
wee

ELIZABETH COATSWORTH

Song of the Rabbits Outside the Tavern

We who play under the pines,
we who dance in the snow
that shines blue in the light of the moon
sometimes halt as we go,
stand with our ears erect,
our noses testing the air,
to gaze at the golden world
behind the windows there.

Suns they have in a cave
and stars each on a tall white stem,
and the thought of fox or night owl
seems never to trouble them.
They laugh and eat and are warm,
their food seems ready at hand,
while hungry out in the cold
we little rabbits stand.

But they never dance as we dance,
they have not the speed nor the grace.
We scorn both the cat and the dog
who lie by their fireplace.
We scorn them licking their paws,
their eyes on an upraised spoon,
we who dance hungry and wild
under a winter's moon.

WILFRED OWEN

Extract from *The Little Mermaid*

Far out at sea, the water is as blue
As cornflowers, and as clear as crystal-core;
But so exceeding deep, no sea-bird's view
Can fathom it, nor men's ropes touch its floor.
Strange, snake-like trees and weeds – the same which
grew

Before dry land with herbs was peopled o'er –
Still sleep in heavy peacefulness down there,
And hold their fluctuous arms towards upper air.

And it is there the Sea-King's nation dwells.
His palace, golden-bright and ruby-red,
Gleams like a crown among those velvet dells.
Pink, shimmering streams of light its windows shed,
Like waterfalls of wine; and pink-white shells,
Like Alpine snows, its lofty roof o'erspread;
Which close and open, close and open wide,
With every ebb and flowing of the tide.

Soldier's Dream

I dreamed kind Jesus fouled the big-gun gears;
And caused a permanent stoppage in all bolts;
And buckled with a smile Mausers and Colts;
And rusted every bayonet with His tears.

And there were no more bombs, of ours or Theirs,
Not even an old flint-lock, nor even a pikel.
But God was vexed, and gave all power to Michael;
And when I woke he'd seen to our repairs.

MORRIS BISHOP

How to Treat Elves

I met an elf-man in the woods,
  The wee-est little elf!
Sitting under a mushroom tall –
  'Twas taller than himself!

'How do you do, little elf,' I said,
  'And what do you do all day?'
'I dance 'n fwolic about,' said he,
  ''N scuttle about and play;

'I s'prise the butterflies, 'n when
  A katydid I see,
"Katy didn't!" I say, and he
  Says "Katy did!" to me!

'I hide behind my mushroom stalk
  When Mister Mole comes froo,
'N only jus' to fwighten him
  I jump out 'n say "Boo!"

"N then I swing on a cobweb swing
  Up in the air so high,
'N the cwickets chirp to hear me sing
  "Upsy-daisy-die!"

''N then I play with the baby chicks,
   I call them, chick chick chick!
'N what do you think of that?' said he.
   I said, 'It makes me sick.

'It gives me sharp and shooting pains
   To listen to such drool.'
I lifted up my foot, and squashed
   The God damn little fool.

W. J. TURNER

India

They hunt, the velvet tigers in the jungle,
The spotted jungle full of shapeless patches –
Sometimes they're leaves, sometimes they're hanging
                                                    flowers,
Sometimes they're hot gold patches of the sun:
They hunt, the velvet tigers in the jungle!

What do they hunt by glimmering pools of water,
By the round silver Moon, the Pool of Heaven –
In the striped grass, amid the barkless trees –
The stars scattered like eyes of beasts above them!

What do they hunt, their hot breath scorching insects,
Insects that blunder blindly in the way,
Vividly fluttering - they also are hunting,
Are glittering with a tiny ecstasy!

The grass is flaming and the trees are growing,
The very mud is gurgling in the pools,
Green toads are watching, crimson parrots flying,
Two pairs of eyes meet one another glowing –
They hunt, the velvet tigers in the jungle.

T. S. ELIOT

Skimbleshanks: The Railway Cat

There's a whisper down the line at 11.39
When the Night Mail's ready to depart,
Saying 'Skimble where is Skimble has he gone to hunt
                    the thimble?
We must find him or the train can't start.'
All the guards and all the porters and the
                    stationmaster's daughters
They are searching high and low,
Saying 'Skimble where is Skimble for unless he's very
                    nimble
Then the Night Mail just can't go.'
At 11.42 then the signal's overdue
And the passengers are frantic to a man –
Then Skimble will appear and he'll saunter to the rear:
He's been busy in the luggage van!
  He gives one flash of his glass-green eyes
    And the signal goes 'All Clear!'

And we're off at last for the northern part
   Of the Northern Hemisphere!

You may say that by and large it is Skimble who's in
                               charge
Of the Sleeping Car Express.
From the driver and the guards to the bagmen playing
                               cards
He will supervise them all, more or less.
Down the corridor he paces and examines all the faces
Of the travellers in the First and in the Third;
He establishes control by a regular patrol
And he'd know at once if anything occurred.
He will watch you without winking and he sees what
                             you are thinking
And it's certain that he doesn't approve
Of hilarity and riot, so the folk are very quiet
When Skimble is about and on the move.
   You can play no pranks with Skimbleshanks!
      He's a Cat that cannot be ignored;
   So nothing goes wrong on the Northern Mail
      When Skimbleshanks is aboard.

Oh it's very pleasant when you have found your little den
With your name written up on the door.
And the berth is very neat with a newly folded sheet
And there's not a speck of dust on the floor.
There is every sort of light – you can make it dark or
                                                    bright:
There's a button that you turn to make a breeze.
There's a funny little basin you're supposed to wash
                                            your face in
And a crank to shut the window if you sneeze.
Then the guard looks in politely and will ask you very
                                            brightly
'Do you like your morning tea weak or strong?'
But Skimble's just behind him and was ready to remind
                                            him,
For Skimble won't let anything go wrong.
   And when you creep into your cosy berth
      And pull up the counterpane,
  You ought to reflect that it's very nice
     To know that you won't be bothered by mice –
  You can leave all that to the Railway Cat,
    The Cat of the Railway Train!

In the watches of the night he is always fresh and bright;
Every now and then he has a cup of tea
With perhaps a drop of Scotch while he's keeping on
                                      the watch,
Only stopping here and there to catch a flea.
You were fast asleep at Crewe and so you never knew
That he was walking up and down the station;
You were sleeping all the while he was busy at Carlisle,
Where he greets the stationmaster with elation.
But you saw him at Dumfries, where he summons the
                                        police
If there's anything they ought to know about:
When you get to Gallowgate there you do not have to
                                        wait –

For Skimbleshanks will help you to get out!
    He gives you a wave of his long brown tail
        Which says: 'I'll see you again!
    You'll meet without fail on the Midnight Mail
        The Cat of the Railway Train.'

EDITH SITWELL

Song XV from *The Sleeping Beauty*

DO, do,
Princess, do,
Like a tree that drips with gold you flow
With beauty ripening very slow.
Soon beneath that peaceful shade
The whole world dreaming will be laid.
Do, do.
Princess, do,
The years like soft winds come and go.

Do, do,
Princess, do,
How river-thick flow your fleeced locks
Like the nymphs' music o'er the rocks . . .
From satyr-haunted caverns drip
These lovely airs on brow and lip.
Do, do,
Princess, do,
Like a tree that drips with gold you flow.

Aubade

Jane, Jane,
Tall as a crane,
The morning light creaks down again;

Comb your cockscomb-ragged hair,
Jane, Jane, come down the stair.

Each dull blunt wooden stalactite
Of rain creaks, hardened by the light,

Sounding like an overtone
From some lonely world unknown.

But the creaking empty light
Will never harden into sight,

Will never penetrate your brain
With overtones like the blunt rain.

The light would show (if it could harden)
Eternities of kitchen garden,

Cockscomb flowers that none will pluck,
And wooden flowers that 'gin to cluck.

In the kitchen you must light
Flames as staring, red and white,

As carrots or as turnips, shining
Where the cold dawn light lies whining.

Cockscomb hair on the cold wind
Hangs limp, turns the milk's weak mind . . .
  Jane, Jane,
  Tall as a crane,
  The morning light creaks down again!

RUPERT BROOKE

These I Have Loved . . .

These I have loved:
      White plates and cups, clean-gleaming,
Ringed with blue lines; and feathery, faery dust;
Wet roofs, beneath the lamp-light; the strong crust
Of friendly bread; and many-tasting food;
Rainbows; and the blue bitter smoke of wood;
And radiant raindrops couching in cool flowers;
And flowers themselves, that sway through sunny hours,
Dreaming of moths that drink them under the moon;
Then, the cool kindliness of sheets, that soon
Smooth away trouble; and the rough male kiss
Of blankets; grainy wood; live hair that is
Shining and free; blue-massing clouds; the keen
Unpassioned beauty of a great machine;
The benison of hot water; furs to touch;
The good smell of old clothes; and other such –
The comfortable smell of friendly fingers,
Hair's fragrance, and the musty reek that lingers
About dead leaves and last year's ferns . . .

                              Dear names,
And thousand other throng to me! Royal flames;
Sweet water's dimpling laugh from tap or spring;
Holes in the ground; and voices that do sing;
Voices in laughter, too; and body's pain,
Soon turned to peace; and the deep-panting train;
Firm sands; the little dulling edge of foam
That browns and dwindles as the wave goes home;
And washen stones, gay for an hour; the cold
Graveness of iron; moist black earthen mould;
Sleep; and high places; footprints in the dew;
And oaks; and brown horse-chestnuts, glossy-new;
And new-peeled sticks; and shining pools on grass; –
All these have been my loves.

E. V. RIEU

The Princess Priscilla

When the Princess Priscilla goes out
There aren't *any* dragons about:
   The dragons decide
   It is better to hide
While the Princess Priscilla is out.

As the Princess Priscilla goes by
There's a kind of gleam in her eye –
   The tail of no dragon
   Could possibly wag on
When the Princess Priscilla goes by.

Sir Smashum Uppe

Good afternoon, Sir Smashum Uppe!
We're having tea: do take a cup!
Sugar and milk? Now let me see –
Two lumps, I think? . . . Good gracious me!
The silly thing slipped off your knee!
Pray don't apologize, old chap:
A very trivial mishap!
So clumsy of you? How absurd!
My dear Sir Smashum, not a word!
Now do sit down and have another,
And tell us all about your brother –
You know, the one who broke his head.
Is the poor fellow still in bed?
A chair – allow me, sir! . . . Great Scott!
That *was* a nasty smash! Eh, what?
Oh, not at all: the chair was old –
Queen Anne, or so we have been told.
We've got at least a dozen more:
Just leave the pieces on the floor.
I want you to admire our view:
Come nearer to the window, do;
And look how beautiful . . . Tut, tut!
You didn't see that it was shut?
I hope you are not badly cut!
Not hurt? A fortunate escape!
Amazing! Not a single scrape!
And now, if you have finished tea,
I fancy you might like to see

A little thing or two I've got.
That china plate? Yes, worth a lot:
A beauty too . . . Ah, there it goes!
I trust it didn't hurt your toes?
Your elbow brushed it off the shelf?
Of course: I've done the same myself.
And now, my dear Sir Smashum – Oh,
You surely don't intend to go?
You *must* be off? Well, come again,
So glad you're fond of porcelain.

Rendez-vous with a Beetle

Meet me in Usk
   And drone to me
Of what a beetle's
   Eye can see
When lamps are lit
And the bats flit
   In Usk
   At dusk.

And tell me if
   A beetle's nose
Detects the perfume
   Of the rose
As gardens fade
And stars invade
   The dusk
   In Usk.

A. A. MILNE

Lines and Squares

Whenever I walk in a London street,
I'm ever so careful to watch my feet;
   And I keep in the squares,
   And the masses of bears,
Who wait at the corners all ready to eat
The sillies who tread on the lines of the street,
   Go back to their lairs,
   And I say to them, 'Bears,
Just look how I'm walking in all the squares!'

And the little bears growl to each other, 'He's mine,
As soon as he's silly and steps on a line.'

And some of the bigger bears try to pretend
That they came round the corner to look for a friend;
And they try to pretend that nobody cares
Whether you walk on the lines or squares.
But only the sillies believe their talk;
It's ever so portant how you walk.

And it's ever so jolly to call out, 'Bears,
Just watch me walking in all the squares!'

Waiting at the Window

These are my two drops of rain
Waiting on the window-pane.

I am waiting here to see
Which the winning one will be.

Both of them have different names.
One is John and one is James.

All the best and all the worst
Comes from which of them is first.

James had just begun to ooze.
He's the one I want to lose.

John is waiting to begin.
He's the one I want to win.

James is going slowly on.
Something sort of sticks to John.

John is moving off at last.
James is going pretty fast.

John is rushing down the pane.
James is going slow again.

James has met a sort of smear.
John is getting very near.

Is he going fast enough?
(James has found a piece of fluff.)

John has hurried quickly by.
(James was talking to a fly.)

John is there, and John has won!
Look! I told you! Here's the sun!

Daffodowndilly

She wore her yellow sun-bonnet,
   She wore her greenest gown;
She turned to the south wind
   And curtsied up and down.
She turned to the sunlight
   And shook her yellow head,
And whispered to her neighbour:
   'Winter is dead.'

ELEANOR FARJEON

Mrs Malone

Mrs Malone
Lived hard by a wood
All on her lonesome
As nobody should.
With her crust on a plate
And her pot on the coal
And none but herself
To converse with, poor soul.
In a shawl and a hood
She got sticks out-o'-door,
On a bit of old sacking
She slept on the floor,
And nobody, nobody
Asked how she fared
Or knew how she managed,
For nobody cared.
   Why make a pother
   About an old crone?
   What for should they bother
   With Mrs Malone?

One Monday in winter
With snow on the ground
So thick that a footstep
Fell without sound,

She heard a faint frostbitten
Peck on the pane
And went to the window
To listen again.
There sat a cock-sparrow
Bedraggled and weak,
With half-open eyelid
And ice on his beak.
She threw up the sash
And she took the bird in,
And mumbled and fumbled it
Under her chin.
   'Ye're all of a smother,
   Ye're fair overblown!
   I've room fer another,'
   Said Mrs Malone.

Come Tuesday while eating
Her dry morning slice
With the sparrow a-picking
('Ain't company nice!')
She heard on her doorpost
A curious scratch,
And there was a cat
With its claw on the latch.
It was hungry and thirsty
And thin as a lath,
It mewed and it mowed
On the slithery path.

She threw the door open
And warmed up some pap,
And huddled and cuddled it
In her old lap.
   'There, there, little brother,
   Ye poor skin-an'-bone,
   There's room fer another,'
   Said Mrs Malone.

Come Wednesday while all of them
Crouched on the mat
With a crumb for the sparrow,
A sip for the cat,
There was wailing and whining
Outside in the wood,
And there sat a vixen
With six of her brood.
She was haggard and ragged
And worn to a shred,
And her half-dozen babies
Were only half-fed,
But Mrs Malone, crying
'My! ain't they sweet!'
Happed them and lapped them
And gave them to eat.
   'You warm yerself, mother,
   Ye're cold as a stone!
   There's room fer another,'
   Said Mrs Malone.

Come Thursday a donkey
Stepped in off the road
With sores on his withers
From bearing a load.
Come Friday when icicles
Pierced the white air
Down from the mountainside
Lumbered a bear.
For each she had something,
If little, to give –
'Lord knows, the poor critters
Must all of 'em live.'
She gave them her sacking,
Her hood and her shawl,
Her loaf and her teapot –
She gave them her all.
   'What with one thing and t'other
   Me fambily's grown,
   And there's room fer another,'
   Said Mrs Malone.

Come Saturday evening
When time was to sup
Mrs Malone
Had forgot to sit up.
The cat said *meeow*,
And the sparrow said *peep*,
The vixen, *she's sleeping*,
The bear, *let her sleep*.
On the back of the donkey
They bore her away,

Through trees and up mountains
Beyond night and day,
Till come Sunday morning
They brought her in state
Through the last cloudbank
As far as the Gate.
  'Who is it,' asked Peter,
  'You have with you there?'
  And donkey and sparrow,
  Cat, vixen and bear

Exclaimed, 'Do you tell us
Up here she's unknown?
It's our mother, God bless us!
It's Mrs Malone
Whose havings were few
And whose holding was small
And whose heart was so big
It had room for us all.'
Then Mrs Malone
Of a sudden awoke,
She rubbed her two eyeballs
And anxiously spoke:
'Where am I, to goodness,
And what do I see?
My dears, let's turn back,
This ain't no place fer me!'
  But Peter said, 'Mother
  Go in to the Throne.
  There's room for another
  One, Mrs Malone.'

The Distance

Over the sounding sea,
Off the wandering sea
I smelt the smell of the distance
And longed for another existence.
Smell of pineapple, maize, and myrrh,
Parrot-feather and monkey-fur,
   Brown spice,
   Blue ice,
Fields of tobacco and tea and rice,

   And soundless snows,
   And snowy cotton,
   Otto of rose
Incense in an ivory palace,
Jungle rivers rich and rotten,
   Slumbering valleys,
   Smouldering mountains,
   Rank morasses
   And frozen fountains,
Black molasses and purple wine,
Coral and pearl and tar and brine,
The smell of panther and polar-bear
   And leopard-lair
   And mermaid-hair
Came from the four-cornered distance,
And I longed for another existence.

The Sounds in the Evening

The sounds in the evening
Go all through the house,
The click of the clock
And the pick of the mouse,
The footsteps of people
Upon the top floor,
The skirts of my mother
That brush by my door,
The crick in the boards,
And the creak of the chairs,
The fluttering murmurs
Outside on the stairs,
The ring at the bell,
The arrival of guests,
The laugh of my father
At one of his jests,
The clashing of dishes
As dinner goes in,
The babble of voices
That distance makes thin,
The mewings of cats
That seem just by my ear,
The hooting of owls
That can never seem near,

The queer little noises
That no one explains –
Till the moon through the slats
Of my window-blind rains,
And the world of my eyes
And my ears melts like steam
As I find in my pillow
The world of my dream.

The Night Will Never Stay

The night will never stay,
  The night will still go by,
Though with a million stars
  You pin it to the sky,
Though you bind it with the blowing wind
  And buckle it with the moon,
The night will slip away
  Like sorrow or a tune.

MARRIOTT EDGAR

The Lion and Albert

There's a famous seaside place called Blackpool,
   That's noted for fresh air and fun,
And Mr and Mrs Ramsbottom
   Went there with young Albert, their son.

A grand little lad was young Albert,
   All dressed in his best; quite a swell
With a stick with an 'orse's 'ead 'andle,
   The finest that Woolworth's could sell.

They didn't think much to the Ocean:
   The waves, they was fiddlin' and small,
There was no wrecks and nobody drownded,
   Fact, nothing to laugh at at all.

So, seeking for further amusement,
   They paid and went into the Zoo,
Where they'd Lions and Tigers and Camels,
   And old ale and sandwiches too.

There were one great big Lion called Wallace;
   His nose were all covered with scars
He lay in a somnolent posture
   With the side of his face on the bars.

Now Albert had heard about Lions,
  How they was ferocious and wild –
To see Wallace lying so peaceful,
  Well, it didn't seem right to the child.

So straightway the brave little feller,
  Not showing a morsel of fear,
Took his stick with its 'orse's 'ead 'andle
  And poked it in Wallace's ear.

You could see that the Lion didn't like it,
  For giving a kind of a roll,
He pulled Albert inside the cage with 'im,
  And swallowed the little lad 'ole.

Then Pa, who had seen the occurrence,
  And didn't know what to do next,
Said 'Mother! Yon Lion's 'et Albert,'
  And Mother said 'Well, I am vexed!'

Then Mr and Mrs Ramsbottom –
  Quite rightly, when all's said and done –
Complained to the Animal Keeper
  That the Lion had eaten their son.

The keeper was quite nice about it;
  He said 'What a nasty mishap.
Are you sure that it's *your* boy he's eaten?'
  Pa said 'Am I sure? There's his cap!'

The manager had to be sent for.
    He came and he said 'What's to do?'
Pa said 'Yon Lion's 'et Albert,
    And 'im in his Sunday clothes, too.'

Then Mother said 'Right's right, young feller;
    I think it's a shame and a sin
For a lion to go and eat Albert,
    And after we've paid to come in.'

The manager wanted no trouble,
    He took out his purse right away,
Saying 'How much to settle the matter?'
    And Pa said 'What do you usually pay?'

But Mother had turned a bit awkward
    When she thought where her Albert had gone.
She said 'No! someone's got to be summonsed' –
    So that was decided upon.

Then off they went to the P'lice Station,
    In front of the Magistrate chap;
They told 'im what happened to Albert,
    And proved it by showing his cap.

The Magistrate gave his opinion
    That no one was really to blame
And he said that he hoped the Ramsbottoms
    Would have further sons to their name.

At that Mother got proper blazing,
   'And thank you, sir, kindly,' said she.
'What, waste all our lives raising children
   To feed ruddy Lions? Not me!'

JAMES STEPHENS

The Snare

I hear a sudden cry of pain!
There is a rabbit in a snare:
Now I hear that cry again,
But I cannot tell from where.

But I cannot tell from where
He is calling out for aid!
Crying on the frightened air,
Making everything afraid!

Making everything afraid!
Wrinkling up his little face!
As he cries again for aid;
And I cannot find the place!

And I cannot find the place
Where his paw is in the snare!
Little One! Oh, Little One!
I am searching everywhere!

VACHEL LINDSAY

The Flower-Fed Buffaloes

The flower-fed buffaloes of the spring
In the days of long ago,
Ranged where the locomotives sing
And the prairie flowers lie low;
The tossing, blooming, perfumed grass
Is swept away by wheat,
Wheels and wheels and wheels spin by
In the spring that still is sweet.
But the flower-fed buffaloes of the spring
Left us long ago.
They gore no more, they bellow no more,
They trundle around the hills no more:
With the Blackfeet, lying low,
With the Pawnees, lying low.

The King of Yellow Butterflies

The King of Yellow Butterflies,
The King of Yellow Butterflies,
The King of Yellow Butterflies,
Now orders forth his men.
He says, 'The time is almost here
When violets bloom again.'
Adown the road the fickle rout
Goes flashing proud and bold,
Adown the road the fickle rout
Goes flashing proud and bold,
Adown the road the fickle rout
Goes flashing proud and bold,
They shiver by the shallow pools,
They shiver by the shallow pools,
They shiver by the shallow pools,
And whimper of the cold.

They drink and drink. A frail pretence!
They love to pose and preen.
Each pool is but a looking glass,
Where their sweet wings are seen.
Each pool is but a looking glass,
Where their sweet wings are seen.
Each pool is but a looking glass,
Where their sweet wings are seen.
Gentlemen adventurers! Gypsies every whit!
They live on what they steal. Their wings
By briars are frayed a bit.
Their loves are light. They have no house.
And if it rains today,
They'll climb into your cattle-shed,
They'll climb into your cattle-shed,
They'll climb into your cattle-shed,
And hide them in the hay,
And hide them in the hay,
And hide them in the hay,
And hide them in the hay.

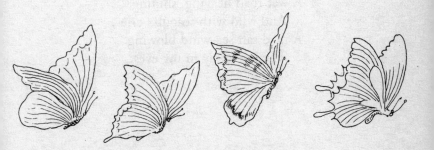

JOHN MASEFIELD

Roadways

One road leads to London,
  One road runs to Wales,
My road leads me seawards
  To the white dipping sails.

One road leads to the river,
  As it goes singing slow;
My road leads to shipping,
  Where the bronzed sailors go.

Leads me, lures me, calls me
  To salt green tossing sea;
A road without earth's road-dust
  Is the right road for me.

A wet road heaving, shining,
  And wild with seagull's cries,
A mad salt sea-wind blowing
  The salt spray in my eyes.

My road calls me, lures me
  West, east, south, and north;
Most roads lead men homewards,
  My road leads me forth.

To add more miles to the tally
  Of grey miles left behind,
In quest of that one beauty
  God put me here to find.

An Old Song Re-Sung

I saw a ship a-sailing, a-sailing, a-sailing,
With emeralds and rubies and sapphires in her hold;
And a bosun in a blue coat bawling at the railing,
Piping through a silver call that had a chain of gold;
The summer wind was failing and the tall ship rolled.

I saw a ship a-steering, a-steering, a-steering,
With roses in red thread worked upon her sails;
With sacks of purple amethysts, the spoils of
                                              buccaneering,
Skins of musky yellow wine, and silks in bales,
Her merry men were cheering, hauling on the brails.

I saw a ship a-sinking, a-sinking, a-sinking,
With glittering sea-water splashing on her decks,
With seamen in her spirit-room singing songs and
                                              drinking,
Pulling claret bottles down, and knocking off the necks,
The broken glass was chinking as she sank among the
                                              wrecks.

EDWARD THOMAS

Snow

In the gloom of whiteness,
In the great silence of snow,
A child was sighing
And bitterly saying: 'Oh,
They have killed a white bird up there on her nest,
The down is fluttering from her breast!'
And still it fell through the dusky brightness
On the child crying for the bird of the snow.

Thaw

Over the land freckled with snow half-thawed
The speculating rooks at their nests cawed
And saw from elm-tops, delicate as flower of grass,
What we below could not see, Winter pass.

Adlestrop

Yes. I remember Adlestrop –
The name, because one afternoon
Of heat the express-train drew up there
Unwontedly. It was late June.

The steam hissed. Someone cleared his throat.
No one left and no one came
On the bare platform. What I saw
Was Adlestrop – only the name

And willows, willow-herb, and grass,
And meadowsweet, and haycocks dry,
No whit less still and lonely fair
Than the high cloudlets in the sky.

And for that minute a blackbird sang
Close by, and round him, mistier,
Farther and farther, all the birds
Of Oxfordshire and Gloucestershire.

ROBERT SERVICE

The Cremation of Sam McGee

There are strange things done in the midnight sun
  By the men who moil for gold;
The Arctic trails have their secret tales
  That would make your blood run cold;
The Northern Lights have seen queer sights,
  But the queerest they ever did see
Was that night on the marge of Lake Lebarge
  I cremated Sam McGee.

Now Sam McGee was from Tennessee, where the
  cotton blooms and blows.
Why he left his home in the South to roam 'round the
  Pole, God only knows.
He was always cold, but the land of gold seemed to
  hold him like a spell;
Though he'd often say in his homely way that 'he'd
  sooner live in hell.'

On a Christmas Day we were mushing our way over
  the Dawson trail.
Talk of your cold! through the parka's fold it stabbed
  like a driven nail.
If our eyes we'd close, then the lashes froze till
  sometimes we couldn't see;
It wasn't much fun, but the only one to whimper was
  Sam McGee.

And that very night, as we lay packed tight in our
  robes beneath the snow.
And the dogs were fed, the stars o'erhead were dancing
  heel and toe,
He turned to me, and 'Cap,' says he, 'I'll cash in this
  trip, I guess;
And if I do, I'm asking that you won't refuse my last
  request.'

Well, he seemed so low that I couldn't say no; then he
  says with a sort of moan:
'It's the cursed cold, and it's got right hold till I'm
  chilled clean through to the bone.
Yet 'tain't being dead – it's my awful dread of the icy
  grave that pains;
So I want you to swear that, foul or fair, you'll cremate
  my last remains.'

A pal's last need is a thing to heed, so I swore I would
    not fail;
And we started on at the streak of dawn; but God! he
    looked ghastly pale.
He crouched on the sleigh, and he raved all day of his
    home in Tennessee;
And before nightfall a corpse was all that was left of
    Sam McGee.

There wasn't a breath in that land of death, and I
    hurried horror-driven,
With a corpse half hid that I couldn't get rid, because
    of a promise given;
It was lashed to the sleigh, and it seemed to say: 'You
    may tax your brawn and brains,
But you promised true, and it's up to you to cremate
    those last remains.'

Now a promise made is a debt unpaid, and the trail
    has its own stern code.
In the days to come, though my lips were dumb, in
    my heart how I cursed that load.
In the long, long night, by the lone firelight, while the
    huskies, round in a ring,
Howled out their woes to the homeless snows – O
    God! how I loathed the thing.

And every day that quiet clay seemed to heavy and
    heavier grow;
And on I went, though the dogs were spent and the
    grub was getting low;
The trail was bad, and I felt half mad, but I swore I
    would not give in;
And I'd often sing to the hateful thing, and it
    hearkened with a grin.

Till I came to the marge of Lake Lebarge, and a derelict
    there lay;
It was jammed in the ice, but I saw in a trice it was
    called the 'Alice May.'
And I looked at it, and I thought a bit, and looked at
    my frozen chum;
Then 'Here,' said I, with a sudden cry, 'is my cre-ma-
    tor-eum.'

Some planks I tore from the cabin floor, and I lit the
    boiler fire;
Some coal I found that was lying around, and I heaped
    the fuel higher;
The flames just soared, and the furnace roared – such a
    blaze you seldom see;
And I burrowed a hole in the glowing coal, and I
    stuffed in Sam McGee.

Then I made a hike, for I didn't like to hear him sizzle
    so;
And the heavens scowled, and the huskies howled, and
    the wind began to blow.
It was icy cold, but the hot sweat rolled down my
    cheeks, and I don't know why;
  And the greasy smoke in an inky cloak went
    streaking down the sky.

I do not know how long in the snow I wrestled with
    grisly fear;
But the stars came out and they danced about ere again
    I ventured near;
I was sick with dread, but I bravely said: 'I'll just take
    a peep inside.
I guess he's cooked, and it's time I looked'; . . . then
    the door I opened wide.

And there sat Sam, looking cool and calm, in the heart
    of the furnace roar;
And he wore a smile you could see a mile, and he said:
    'Please close that door.
It's fine in here, but I greatly fear you'll let in the cold
    and storm –
Since I left Plumtree, down in Tennessee, it's the first
    time I've been warm.

> *There are strange things done in the midnght sun*
>   *By the men who moil for gold;*
> *The Arctic trails have their secret tales*
>   *That would make your blood run cold;*
> *The Northern Lights have seen queer sights,*
>   *But the queerest they ever did see*
> *Was that night on the marge of Lake Lebarge*
>   *I cremated Sam McGee.*

Old David Smail

He dreamed away his hours in school;
He sat with such an absent air,
The master reckoned him a fool,
And gave him up in dull despair.

When other lads were making hay
You'd find him loafing by the stream;
He'd take a book and slip away,
And just pretend to fish . . . and dream.

His brothers passed him in the race;
They climbed the hill and clinched the prize.
He did not seem to heed, his face
Was tranquil as the evening skies.

He lived apart, he spoke with few,
Abstractedly through life he went;
Oh, what he dreamed of no one knew,
And yet he seemed to be content.

I see him now, so old and grey.
His eyes with inward vision dim;
And though he faltered on the way,
Somehow I almost envied him.

At last beside his bed I stood:
'And is Life done so soon?' he sighed;
'It's been so rich, so full, so good,
I've loved it all . . .' – and so he died.

HARRY GRAHAM

Politeness

My cousin John was most polite;
He led shortsighted Mrs Bond,
By accident, one winter's night
Into a village pond.
Her life perhaps he might have saved
But how genteelly he behaved!

Each time she rose and waved to him
He smiled and bowed and doffed his hat;
Thought he, although I cannot swim,
At least I can do that –
And when for the third time she sank
He stood bareheaded on the bank.

Be civil, then, to young and old;
Especially to persons who
Possess a quantity of gold
Which they might leave to you.
The more they have, it seems to me,
The more polite you ought to be.

Uncle

Uncle, whose inventive brains
Kept evolving aeroplanes,
Fell from an enormous height
On my garden lawn, last night.
  Flying is a fatal sport,
  Uncle wrecked the tennis-court.

ROBERT FROST

The Last Word of a Bluebird
(as Told to a Child)

As I went out a Crow
In a low voice said, 'Oh,
I was looking for you.
How do you do?
I just came to tell you
To tell Lesley (will you?)
That her little Bluebird
Wanted me to bring word
That the north wind last night
That made the stars bright
And made ice on the trough
Almost made him cough
His tail feathers off.
He just had to fly!
But he sent her Goodbye
And said to be good,
And wear her red hood,
And look for skunk tracks
In the snow with an axe –
And do everything!
And perhaps in the spring
He would come back and sing.'

Stopping by Woods on a Snowy Evening

Whose woods these are I think I know.
His house is in the village, though;
He will not see me stopping here
To watch his woods fill up with snow.

My little horse must think it queer
To stop without a farmhouse near
Between the woods and frozen lake
The darkest evening of the year.

He gives his harness bells a shake
To ask if there is some mistake.
The only other sound's the sweep
Of easy wind and downy flake.

The woods are lovely, dark, and deep,
But I have promises to keep,
And miles to go before I sleep,
And miles to go before I sleep.

A Minor Bird

I have wished a bird would fly away,
And not sing by my house all day;

Have clapped my hands at him from the door
When it seemed as if I could bear no more.

The fault must partly have been in me.
The bird was not to blame for his key.

And of course there must be something wrong
In wanting to silence any song.

G. K. CHESTERTON

The Donkey

When fishes flew and forests walked,
 And figs grew upon thorn,
Some moments when the moon was blood,
 Then surely I was born;

With monstrous head and sickening cry
 And ears like errant wings,
The devil's walking parody
 On all four-footed things.

The tattered outlaw of the earth,
 Of ancient crooked will;
Starve, scourge, deride me: I am dumb,
 I keep my secret still.

Fools! For I also had my hour;
 One far fierce hour and sweet:
There was a shout about my ears,
 And palms before my feet.

WALTER DE LA MARE

Tom's Angel

No one was in the fields
But me and Polly Flint,
When, like a giant across the grass,
The flaming angel went.

It was budding time in May,
And green as green could be,
And all in his height he went along
Past Polly Flint and me.

We'd been playing in the woods,
And Polly up, and ran,
And hid her face, and said,
'Tom! Tom! The Man! The Man!'

And I up-turned; and there,
Like flames across the sky,
With wings all bristling, came
The Angel striding by.

And a chaffinch overhead
Kept whistling in the tree
While the Angel, blue as fire, came on
Past Polly Flint and me.

And I saw his hair, and all
The ruffling of his hem,
As over the clovers his bare feet
Trod without stirring them.

Polly – she cried; and, oh!
We ran, until the lane
Turned by the miller's roaring wheel,
And we were safe again.

Before Dawn

Dim-berried is the mistletoe
With globes of sheenless grey,
The holly mid ten thousand thorns
Smoulders its fires away;
And in the manger Jesu sleeps
    This Christmas Day.

Bull unto bull with hollow throat
Makes echo every hill,
Cold sheep in pastures thick with snow
The air with bleatings fill;
While of his mother's heart this Babe
    Takes His sweet will.

All flowers and butterflies lie hid,
The blackbird and the thrush
Pipe but a little as they flit
Restless from bush to bush;
Even to the robin Gabriel hath
    Cried soffly, 'Hush!'

Now night's astir with burning stars
In darkness of the snow;
Burdened with frankincense and myrrh
And gold the Strangers go
Into a dusk where one dim lamp
    Burns faintly, Lo!

No snowdrop yet its small head nods,
In winds of winter drear;
No lark at casement in the sky
Sings matins shrill and clear;
Yet in this frozen mirk the Dawn
    Breathes, Spring is here!

A Robin

Ghost-grey the fall of night,
    Ice-bound the lane,
Lone in the dying light
    Flits he again;
Lurking where shadows steal,
Perched in his coat of blood,
Man's homestead at his heel,
    Death-still the wood.

The Listeners

'Is there anybody there?' said the Traveller,
  Knocking on the moonlit door;
And his horse in the silence champed the grasses
  Of the forest's ferny floor:
And a bird flew up out of the turret,
  Above the Traveller's head:
And he smote upon the door again a second time;
  'Is there anybody there?' he said.
But no one descended to the Traveller;
  No head from the leaf-fringed sill
Leaned over and looked into his grey eyes,
  Where he stood perplexed and still.
But only a host of phantom listeners
  That dwelt in the lone house then
Stood listening in the quiet of the moonlight
  To that voice from the world of men:
Stood thronging the faint moonbeams on the dark stair
  That goes down to the empty hall,
Hearkening in an air stirred and shaken
  By the lonely Traveller's call.
And he felt in his heart their strangeness,
  Their stillness answering his cry,
While his horse moved, cropping the dark turf,
  'Neath the starred and leafy sky;
For he suddenly smote on the door, even
  Louder, and lifted his head: –
'Tell them I came, and no one answered,
  That I kept my word,' he said.

Never the least stir made the listeners,
  Though every word he spake
Fell echoing through the shadowiness of the still house
  From the one man left awake:
Ay, they heard his foot upon the stirrup,
  And the sound of iron on stone,
And how the silence surged softly backward,
  When the plunging hoofs were gone.

The Linnet

Upon this leafy bush
　　With thorns and roses in it,
Flutters a thing of light,
　　A twittering linnet,
And all the throbbing world
　　Of dew and sun and air
By this small parcel of life
　　Is made more fair:
As if each bramble-spray
　　And mounded gold-wreathed furze,
Harebell and little thyme,
　　Were only hers;
As if this beauty and grace
　　Did to one bird belong,
And, at a flutter of wing,
　　Might vanish in song.

The Scarecrow

All winter through I bow my head
   Beneath the driving rain;
The North Wind powders me with snow
   And blows me black again;
At midnight in a maze of stars
   I flame with glittering rime,
And stand, above the stubble, stiff
   As mail at morning-prime.
But when that child, called Spring, and all
   His host of children, come,
Scattering their buds and dew upon
   These acres of my home,
Some rapture in my rags awakes;
   I lift void eyes and scan
The skies for crows, those ravening foes,
   Of my strange master, Man.
I watch him striding lank behind
   His clashing team, and know
Soon will the wheat swish body high
   Where once lay sterile snow;
Soon shall I gaze across a sea
   Of sun-begotten grain,
Which my unflinching watch hath sealed
   For harvest once again.

W. H. DAVIES

The Blind Boxer

He goes with basket and slow feet,
To sell his nuts from street to street;
The very terror of his kind,
Till blackened eyes had made him blind.
For this is Boxer Bob, the man
That had hard muscles, harder than
A schoolboy's bones; who held his ground
When six tall bullies sparred around.
Small children now, that have no grace,
Can steal his nuts before his face;
And when he threatens with his hands,
Mock him two feet from where he stands;
Mock him who could some years ago
Have leapt five feet to strike a blow.
Poor Bobby, I remember when
Thou wert a god to drunken men;
But now they push thee off, or crack
Thy nuts and give no money back.
They swear they'll strike thee in the face,
Dost thou not hurry from that place.
Such are the men that once would pay
To keep thee drunk from day to day.
With all thy strength and cunning skill,
Thy courage, lasting breath and will,

Thou'rt helpless now; a little ball,
No bigger than a cherry small,
Has now refused to guide and lead
Twelve stone of strong hard flesh that need
But that ball's light to make thee leap
And strike these cowards down like sheep.
Poor helpless Bobby, blind; I see
Thy working face and pity thee.

The Happy Child

I saw this day sweet flowers grow thick –
But not one like the child did pick.

I heard the pack-hounds in green park –
But no dog like the child heard bark.

I heard this day bird after bird –
But not one like the child has heard.

A hundred butterflies saw I –
But not one like the child saw fly.

I saw the horses roll in grass –
But no horse like the child saw pass.

My world this day has lovely been –
But not like what the child has seen.

HILAIRE BELLOC

Rebecca
(Who Slammed Doors for Fun and Perished Miserably)

A Trick that everyone abhors
In Little Girls is slamming Doors.
A Wealthy Banker's Little Daughter
Who lived in Palace Green, Bayswater
(By name Rebecca Offendort),
Was given to this Furious Sport.

She would deliberately go
And Slam the door like Billy-Ho!
To make her Uncle Jacob start.
She was not really bad at heart,
But only rather rude and wild;
She was an aggravating child.

It happened that a Marble Bust
Of Abraham was standing just
Above the Door this little Lamb
Had carefully prepared to Slam,
And Down it came! It knocked her flat!
It laid her out! She looked like that!

*   *   *   *   *   *   *   *

Her Funeral Sermon (which was long
And followed by a Sacred Song)
Mentioned her Virtues, it is true,
But dwelt upon her Vices, too,
And showed the Dreadful End of One
Who goes and slams the Door for Fun.

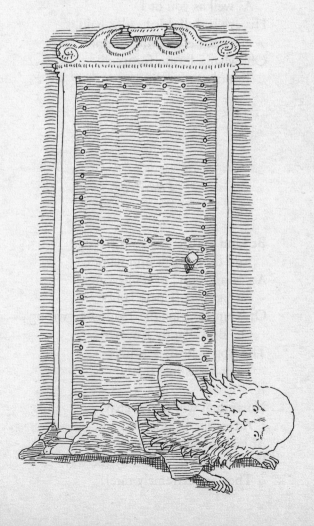

The Vulture

The Vulture eats between his meals,
    And that's the reason why
He very, very rarely feels
    As well as you or I.
His eye is dull, his head is bald,
    His neck is growing thinner.
Oh, what a lesson for us all
    To only eat at dinner.

The Frog

Be kind and tender to the Frog,
    And do not call him names,
As 'Slimy-skin', or 'Polly-wog',
    Or likewise 'Uncle James',
Or 'Gape-a-grin', or 'Toad-gone-wrong',
    Or 'Billy-Bandy Knees':
The frog is justly sensitive
    To epithets like these.

No animal will more repay
    A treatment kind and fair,
At least so lonely people say
Who keep a frog (and by the way,
    They are extremely rare).

The Microbe

The Microbe is so very small
You cannot make him out at all,
But many sanguine people hope
To see him through a microscope.
His jointed tongue that lies beneath
A hundred curious rows of teeth;
His seven tufted tails with lots
Of lovely pink and purple spots,
On each of which a pattern stands,
Composed of forty separate bands;
His eyebrows of a tender green;
All these have never yet been seen –
But Scientists, who ought to know,
Assure us that they must be so . . .
Oh! let us never, never doubt
What nobody is sure about!

Jack and His Pony, Tom

Jack had a little pony – Tom;
He frequently would take it from
The stable where it used to stand
And give it sugar with his hand.

He also gave it oats and hay
And carrots twenty times a day
And grass in basketfuls, and greens,
And swedes and mangolds, also beans,
And patent foods from various sources
And bread (which isn't good for horses)
And chocolate and apple-rings
And lots and lots of other things
The most of which do not agree
With Polo Ponies such as he.
And all in such a quantity
As ruined his digestion wholly
And turned him from a Ponopoly
 – I mean a Polo Pony – into
A case that clearly must be seen to.
Because he swelled and swelled and swelled.
Which, when the kindly boy beheld,
He gave him medicine by the pail
And malted milk, and nutmeg ale,
And yet it only swelled the more
Until its stomach touched the floor.
And when it heaved and groaned as well
And staggered, till at last it fell
And found it could not rise again.

Jack wept and prayed – but all in vain.
The pony died, and as it died
Kicked him severely in his side.

Moral

Kindness to animals should be
Attuned to their brutality.

MARY GILMORE

The Wild Horses

Let the dark mountain shake to the thunder
  Where the wild horses trample the fern,
Let the deep vales re-echo and wonder,
  When, like an eddy, they circle and turn!
Watch the lithe motion
Run free as an ocean,
Never has man laid a hand on a head;
Never a halter
Had bid a step falter,
Never a crest bent down to be led!

Mark, in their starting, the pride of their bearing.
  Swift wheel the leaders, each in his place;
Snorting, they stare at us, timid and daring,
  Ere with a whirl they are off at a race.
O, the wild sally,
As, down through the valley,
Turn they again to the mountains they know;
Chased and the chaser
Outstretched like a racer,
Where, as the wind, unconquered they go! . . .

What though the pommel scarce keep you from
                                            reeling;
   What though the breath be almost a cry;
What though all turn in a dream that is stealing
   Sense from intention and light from the eye –
Follow them, follow,
By height and by hollow;
Follow them, follow, whatever the course!
Soon will the wonder
Die out with the thunder,
Soon will the mountain forget the wild horse.

W. B. YEATS

Two Songs of a Fool

I

A speckled cat and a tame hare
Eat at my hearthstone
And sleep there;
And both look up to me alone
For learning and defence
As I look up to Providence.

I start out of my sleep to think
Some day I may forget
Their food and drink;
Or, the house door left unshut,
The hare may run till it's found
The horn's sweet note and the tooth of the hound.

I bear a burden that might well try
Men that do all by rule,
And what can I
That am a wandering-witted fool
But pray to God that He ease
My great responsibilities?

II

I slept on my three-legged stool by the fire,
The speckled cat slept on my knee;
We never thought to enquire
Where the brown hare might be,
And whether the door were shut.
Who knows how she drank the wind
Stretched up on two legs from the mat,
Before she had settled her mind
To drum with her heel and to leap?
Had I but awakened from sleep
And called her name, she had heard,
It may be, and had not stirred,
That now, it may be, has found
The horn's sweet note and the tooth of the hound.

The Song of Wandering Aengus

I went out to the hazel wood,
Because a fire was in my head,
And cut and peeled a hazel wand,
And hooked a berry to a thread;
And when white moths were on the wing,
And moth-like stars were flickering out,
I dropped the berry in a stream
And caught a little silver trout.

When I laid it on the floor
I went to blow the fire aflame,
But something rustled on the floor,
And some one called me by my name.
It had become a glimmering girl
With apple blossom in her hair
Who called me by my name and ran
And faded through the brightening air.

Though I am old with wandering
Through hollow lands and hilly lands,
I will find out where she has gone,
And kiss her lips and take her hands;
And walk among long dappled grass,
And pluck till time and times are done
The silver apples of the moon,
The golden apples of the sun.

RUDYARD KIPLING

A Smuggler's Song

If you wake at midnight and hear a horse's feet,
Don't go drawing back the blind, or looking in the
$$\text{street,}$$
Them that asks no questions isn't told a lie.
Watch the wall, my darling, while the Gentlemen go by!
     Five and twenty ponies,
     Trotting through the dark –
     Brandy for the Parson,
     Baccy for the Clerk;
     Laces for a lady; letters for a spy,
And watch the wall, my darling, while the Gentlemen
          go by!

Running round the woodlump if you chance to find
Little barrels, roped and tarred, all full of brandy-wine;
Don't you shout to come and look, nor take 'em for
          your play;
Put the brushwood back again, – and they'll be gone
          next day!

If you see the stableyard setting open wide;
If you see a tired horse lying down inside;
If your mother mends a coat cut about and tore;
If the lining's wet and warm – don't you ask no more!

If you meet King George's men, dressed in blue and red,
You be careful what you say, and mindful what is said.
If they call you 'pretty maid', and chuck you 'neath the
                                            chin,
Don't you tell where no one is, nor yet where no one's
                                            been!

Knocks and footsteps round the house – whistles after
                                            dark –
You've no call for running out till the housedogs bark.
Trusty's here and Pincher's here, and see how dumb
                                        they lie –
They don't fret to follow when the Gentlemen go by!

If you do as you've been told, likely there's a chance,
You'll be give a dainty doll, – all the way from France,
With a cap of Valenciennes, and a velvet hood –
A present from the Gentlemen, along o' being good!
        Five and twenty ponies,
        Trotting through the dark –
        Brandy for the Parson,
        Baccy for the Clerk;
Them that asks no questions isn't told a lie –
Watch the wall, my darling, while the Gentlemen go by!

The Way Through the Woods

They shut the road through the woods
Seventy years ago.
Weather and rain have undone it again,
And now you would never know
There was once a road through the woods
Before they planted the trees.
It is underneath the coppice and heath
And the thin anemones.
Only the keeper sees
That, where the ring-dove broods,
And the badgers roll at ease,
There was once a road through the woods.

Yet, if you enter the woods
Of a summer evening late,
When the night-air cools on the trout-ringed pools
Where the otter whistles his mate,
(They fear not men in the woods,
Because they see so few.)
You will hear the beat of a horse's feet,
And the swish of a skirt in the dew,
Steadily cantering through
The misty solitudes,
As though they perfectly knew
The old lost road through the woods . . .
But there is no road through the woods.

A. B. (BANJO) PATERSON

Waltzing Matilda

Oh! there once was a swagman camped by a Billabong
   Under the shade of a Coolabah tree;
And he sang as he looked at his old billy boiling,
'Who'll come a-waltzing Matilda with me?'

Who'll come a-waltzing Matilda, my darling,
   Who'll come a-waltzing Matilda with me?
Waltzing Matilda and leading a water-bag –
   Who'll come a-waltzing Matilda with me?

Down came a jumbuck to drink at the water-hole,
   Up jumped the swagman and grabbed him in glee;
And he sang as he stowed him away in his tucker-bag,
   'You'll come a-waltzing Matilda with me!'

Down came the Squatter a-riding his thoroughbred;
   Down came Policemen – one, two, and three.
'Whose is the jumbuck you've got in the tucker-bag?
   You'll come a-waltzing Matilda with me.'

But the swagman, he up and he jumped in the water
                        hole,
   Drowning himself by the Coolabah tree;
And his ghost may be heard as it sings in the Billabong,
   'Who'll come a-waltzing Matilda with me?'

Buffalo Country

Out where the grey streams glide,
Sullen and deep and slow,
And the alligators slide
From the mud to the depths below
Or drift on the stream like a floating death,
Where the fever comes on the South wind's breath,
There is the buffalo.

Out on the big lagoons,
Where the Regia lilies float,
And the Nankin heron croons
With a deep ill-omened note,
In the ooze and the mud of the swamps below
Lazily wallows the buffalo,
Buried to nose and throat.

From the hunter's gun he hides
In the jungles dark and damp,
Where the slinking dingo glides
And the flying foxes camp;
Hanging like myriad fiends in line
Where the trailing creepers twist and twine
And the sun is a sluggish lamp.

On the edge of the rolling plains
Where the coarse cane grasses swell,
Lush with the tropic rains
In the noon-tide's drowsy spell,

Slowly the buffalo grazes through
Where the brolgas dance, and the jabiru
Stands like a sentinel.

All that the world can know
Of the wild and the weird is here,
Where the black men come and go
With their boomerang and spear,
And the wild duck darken the evening sky
As they fly to their nests in the reedbeds high
When the tropic night is near.

OLIVER HERFORD

A Tragedy in Rhyme

There was a man upon a time
Who could not speak except in rhyme.
He could not voice his smallest wish,
He could not order soup or fish,
He could not hail a passing car,
He could not ask for a cigar, –
And let a rhymeless sentence mar
His speech. He could not vent despair,
Anger, or rage – he could not swear,
He could not even have his say
On common topics of the day.
The dreadful cold – the awful heat,
The rise in coal, the fall in wheat,
He could not rise to give his seat
In crowded car to maiden sweet,
Or buy a paper in the street, –
Except in measured, rhyming feet.
'He must have been a man of means!
In this, the age of magazines!'
I hear you say. Ah, reader, wait
Till you have heard his awful fate.
You will not then expatiate
Upon his fortune. –

Well, one night
A burglar came, and at the sight,
The rhymester took a fearful fright.
The only avenue for flight
Was up the chimney; here he climbed
Until he stuck, and then he rhymed
As follows: –
   'Goodness gracious me!
I'm stuck as tight as tight can be!
Oh, dear, I'm in an awful plight.
I cannot budge to left or right,
Or up or down this awful chimney!'
Then he *was* stuck; had he said 'Jimm'ny!'
It would have saved him many a pang.
But no! he could not stoop to slang.
In vain he writhed and racked his brain
For rhymes to 'chimney'.
   It was plain
He *had* to rhyme – for should he cease
He must forever hold his peace.
He tried to shout, he tried to call.
The truth fell on him like a pall.
There isn't any rhyme at all
To 'chimney'. –
   When they searched the room
They found it silent as a tomb.
For years they advertised in vain
They never heard of him again.

A. E. HOUSMAN

The Grizzly Bear

The Grizzly Bear is huge and wild;
He has devoured the infant child.
The infant child is not aware
He has been eaten by the bear.

When Green Buds Hang

When green buds hang in the elm like dust
    And sprinkle the lime like rain,
Forth I wander, forth I must,
    And drink of life again.
Forth I must by hedgerow bowers
    To look at the leaves uncurled,
And stand in the fields where cuckoo-flowers
    Are lying about the world.

KATHARINE PYLE

The Toys Talk of the World

'I should like,' said the vase from the china-store,
'To have seen the world a little more.

When they carried me here I was wrapped up tight,
But they say it is really a lovely sight.'

'Yes,' said a little plaster bird,
'That is exactly what *I* have heard;

'There are thousands of trees, and oh, what a sight
It must be when the candles are all alight.'

The fat top rolled on his other side:
'It is not in the least like that,' he cried.

'Except myself and the kite and ball,
None of you know of the world at all.

'There are houses, and pavements hard and red,
And everything spins around,' he said;

'Sometimes it goes slowly, and sometimes fast,
And often it stops with a bump at last.'

The wooden donkey nodded his head:
'I had heard the world was like that,' he said.

The kite and the ball exchanged a smile,
But they did not speak; it was not worth while.

LAURA E. RICHARDS

The Mouse

I'm only a poor little mouse, ma'am!
I live in the wall of your house, ma'am!
With a fragment of cheese, and a *very* few peas,
I was having a little carouse, ma'am!

No mischief at all I intend, ma'am!
I hope you will act as my friend, ma'am!
If my life you should take, many hearts it would break,
And the trouble would be without end, ma'am!

My wife lives in there in the crack, ma'am!
She's waiting for me to come back, ma'am!
She hoped I might find a bit of a rind,
For the children their dinner do lack, ma'am!

'Tis hard living there in the wall, ma'am!
For plaster and mortar will pall, ma'am,
On the minds of the young, and when specially hung-
Ry, upon their poor father they'll fall, ma'am!

I never was given to strife, ma'am!
(*Don't* look at that terrible knife, ma'am!)
The noise overhead that disturbs you in bed,
'Tis the rats, I will venture my life, ma'am!

In your eyes I see mercy, I'm sure, ma'am!
Oh, there's no need to open the door, ma'am!
I'll slip through the crack, and I'll never come back,
Oh, I'll NEVER come back any more, ma'am!

Why Does It Snow?

'Why does it snow? Why does it snow?'
The children come crowding around me to know.
I said to my nephew, I said to my niece,
'It's just the old woman a-plucking her geese.

> With her riddle cum dinky dido,
> With her riddle cum dinky dee.

The old woman sits on a pillowy cloud,
She calls to her geese, and they come in a crowd;
A cackle, a wackle, a hiss and a cluck,
And then the old woman begins for to pluck.

> With her riddle cum dinky dido,
> With her riddle cum dinky dee.

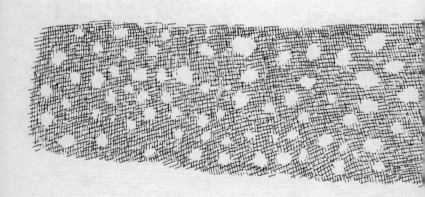

The feathers go gluttering up in the air,
Until the poor geese are entirely bare;
A toddle, a waddle, a hiss and a cluck,
'You may grow some more if you have the good luck!'

     With your riddle cum dinky dido,
     With your riddle cum dinky dee.

The feathers go swirling around and around,
Then whirlicking, twirlicking, sink to the ground;
The farther they travel, the colder they grow,
And when they get down here, they've turned into
                                 snow.

     With their riddle cum dinky dido,
     With their riddle cum dinky dee.

THOMAS HARDY

Snow in the Suburbs

Every branch big with it,
Bent every twig with it;
Every fork like a white web-foot;
Every street and pavement mute:
Some flakes have lost their way, and grope back
                           upward, when
Meeting those meandering down they turn and descend
                                 again.
The palings are glued together like a wall,
And there is no waft of wind with the fleecy fall.

A sparrow enters the tree,
Whereon immediately
A snow-lump thrice his own slight size
Descends on him and showers his head and eyes,
And overturns him,
And near inurns him,
And lights on a nether twig, when its brush
Starts off a volley of other lodging lumps with a rush.

The steps are a blanched slope,
Up which, with feeble hope,
A black cat comes, wide-eyed and thin;
And we take him in.

Weathers

This is the weather the cuckoo likes,
    And so do I;
When showers betumble the chestnut spikes,
    And nestlings fly:
And the little brown nightingale bills his best,
And they sit outside at 'The Traveller's Rest',
And maids come forth sprig-muslin drest,
And citizens dream of the south and west,
    And so do I.

This is the weather the shepherd shuns,
    And so do I;
When beeches drip in brown and duns,
    And thresh, and ply;
And hill-hid tides throb, throe on throe,
And meadow rivulets overflow,
And drops on gate-bars hang in a row,
And rooks in families homeward go,
    And so do I.

Paying Calls

I went by footpath and by stile
　Beyond where bustle ends,
Strayed here a mile and there a mile
　And called upon some friends.

On certain ones I had not seen
　For years past did I call,
And then on others who had been
　The oldest friends of all.

It was the time of midsummer
　When they had used to roam;
But now, though tempting was the air,
　I found them all at home.

I spoke to one and other of them
　By mound and stone and tree
Of things we had done ere days were dim,
　But they spoke not to me.

Transformations

Portion of this yew
Is a man my grandsire knew,
Bosomed here at its foot:
This branch may be his wife,
A ruddy human life
Now turned to a green shoot.

These grasses must be made
Of her who often prayed
Last century, for repose;
And the fair girl long ago
Whom I often tried to know
May be entering this rose.

So, they are not underground,
But as nerves and veins abound
In the growths of upper air,
And they feel the sun and rain,
And the energy again
That made them what they were!

Index of Poets

INDEX OF POEMS

INDEX OF FIRST LINES

BIOGRAPHICAL NOTES

JOHN AGARD was born in 1949 in Guyana. He has lived in England since 1977. A popular performer of poetry for children and adults, his publications include *Limbo Dancer in Dark Glasses* (1983) and, for children, *Say It Again, Granny!* (1986), *Laughter is an Egg* (1990), *Get Back, Pimple* (1996) and *We Animals Would Like a Word with You* (1996).

ALLAN AHLBERG was born in 1938 in London. He writes poetry and fiction for children, and many of his books are illustrated by his late wife, Janet Ahlberg. His collections of poems include *Please Mrs Butler* (1983) and *Heard it in the Playground* (1989).

W. H. (WYSTAN HUGH) AUDEN (1907-73) was born in York. He was the pre-eminent British poet of the 1930s. He emigrated to New York in 1939 and became an American citizen in 1946. Major publications include *Poems* (1930) and *The Shield of Achilles* (1955). His *Collected Shorter Poems: 1927–1957* appeared in 1966.

GEORGE BARKER (1913-1991) was born in Essex but grew up in a tenement in Chelsea. He was associated with Dylan Thomas and the neo-Romantic movement of the 1940s. Among his many books of poetry since then are *Collected Poems* (1987) and three collections for children, including *To Aylsham Fair* (1970).

HILAIRE BELLOC (1870-1953) was born in France of Anglo-French parentage. He was brought up in England. An eminent novelist and man of letters in his day, he is remembered chiefly for his books of children's verse. These include *The Bad Child's Book of Beasts* (1896) and *Cautionary Tales for Children* (1907).

JAMES BERRY was born in 1924 in Jamaica. Since 1948 he has lived in England. He was editor of the anthology of Afro-Caribbean poetry *News for Babylon* (1984). His own poetry collections include *Lucy's Letters and Loving* (1982). For children, he has written the picture book *Celebration Song* (1994) and poetry collections including *When I Dance* (1988) and *Playing a Dazzler* (1996).

SIR JOHN BETJEMAN (1906-84) was born in London. He became a schoolteacher and later wrote books on architecture and the English landscape. His poems reflect similar interests. In 1972 he was appointed Poet Laureate. His publications include *Collected Poems* (1962) and his verse-autobiography *Summoned by Bells* (1960).

MORRIS BISHOP (1893-1973) was born in New York State. He was Professor of Romance Languages at Cornell University from 1921 to 1960. He wrote light verse for *The New Yorker* and other magazines. His books include *Spilt Milk* (1942) and the posthumous selection *The Best of Bishop* (1980).

N. M. (NIELS MOGENS) BODECKER was born in 1922 in Copenhagen. He published poems in Danish before emigrating to the United States in 1952. He illustrated children's books and later began to write for children. Publications include *Let's Marry Said the Cherry and Other Nonsense Poems* (1974) and *Snowman Sniffles and Other Verse* (1983).

RUPERT BROOKE (1887-1915) was born in Rugby. He was prominent among the Georgian poets before the outbreak of the First World War. He served on the Western Front and later died of blood-poisoning near the Greek island of Scyros, where he is buried. *Collected Poems* appeared in 1918.

ALAN BROWNJOHN was born in 1931 in London. He worked as a teacher and lecturer until 1979, when he became a full-time writer. With Sandy Brownjohn, his wife, he has edited several teaching anthologies called *Meet and Write*. Other publications include *Collected Poems: 1952–1988* (1988) and, for children, *Brownjohn's Beasts* (1970).

SYDNEY CARTER was born in 1915 in London. He has published poetry, including *The Two-Way Clock* (1974), but is best known as a composer of folk-songs and hymns. *Green Print for Song* (1974) is a collection of his lyrics and music.

CHARLES CAUSLEY was born in 1917 in Cornwall, where he continues to live. He retired from teaching in 1976 to become a full-time writer. Among his collections of poetry for children are *Figure of 8* (1969), *Figgie Hobbin* (1970), *Early in the Morning: A Collection of New Poems* (1986) and *Going to the Fair: Selected Poems for Children* (1994). He was awarded a CBE in 1986.

G. K. (GILBERT KING) CHESTERTON (1874-1936) was born in London. He was a prolific man of letters and a Catholic apologist. He also created the popular detective Father Brown, who first appeared in *The Innocence of Father Brown* (1911). His poetry publications include *The Wild Knight* (1900) and *Poems* (1915).

LEONARD CLARK (1905-81) was born in Guernsey. He worked as an Inspector of Schools until retirement in 1970. He wrote poetry for adults and children. Among his children's books are *Collected Poems and Verses for Children* (1975) and *The Singing Time* (1980).

ELIZABETH COATSWORTH (1893-1986) was born in Buffalo, New York. She wrote numerous stories for children and also published verse and fiction for adults. Among her poetry collections for children are *Night and the Cat* (1950) and *The Peaceable Kingdom and Other Poems* (1958).

E. E. (EDWARD ESTLIN) CUMMINGS (1894-1962) was born in Cambridge, Massachusetts. He served in the Ambulance Corps during the First World War and was interned in France. His poetry, which makes inventive use of typography, is collected in *Complete Poems* (1968). *Hist Whist* (1983) is a selection he made for children.

ROALD DAHL (1916-90) was born in Glamorgan, Wales, of Norwegian parents. His first children's story, *The Gremlins* (1943), was illustrated by the Walt Disney Studio. *The BFG* (1982) and *Revolting Rhymes* (1982) are among his many highly successful books for children. *Matilda* (1988) became a major feature film of the same name. Of his adult fiction, *Tales of the Unexpected* (1979) became a television series.

W. H. (WILLIAM HENRY) DAVIES (1871-1940) was born in
Newport, Wales. His *Autobiography of a Super-Tramp* (1908)
recounts his adventurous life until a train accident in Canada caused
him to lose a leg. Thereafter he settled down to write the poetry
collected in *The Complete Poems of W. H. Davies* (1963).

WALTER DE LA MARE (1873-1956) was born in Kent. He
worked as a bookkeeper until 1908, when he was granted a Civil
List pension. *The Listeners and Other Poems* (1912) brought him
enduring fame. Later publications include the anthology for young
readers *Come Hither* (1923) and *Poems for Children* (1930).

MICHAEL DUGAN was born in 1947 in Melbourne, Australia. He
has edited various publications, including the children's magazine
Puffinalia. Among his books of poems for adults are *Missing People*
(1970) and, for children, *Stuff and Nonsense* (1974) and *Nonsense
Places* (1976).

MARRIOT EDGAR (1880-1951) was born in Kirkcudbright,
Scotland. He was a music-hall actor who wrote for the stage,
including a musical comedy *Jill Darling!* (1937). Two of his
monologues, popularized by Stanley Holloway, have been reissued
as children's books, *The Lion and Albert* (1978) and *Albert Comes
Back* (1980).

RICHARD EDWARDS was born in 1949 in Kent. He has lived in
Italy and France and is a part-time teacher. His books of children's
verse include *The Word Party* (1986), *A Mouse in my Roof* (1988), *If
Only* (1990), *The House that Caught a Cold* (1991) and *Leopards on
Mars* (1993).

T. S. (THOMAS STEARNS) ELIOT (1888-1965) was born in St
Louis, Missouri. From 1914 he lived in England and, in 1925, he
became a director of Faber. He received the Nobel Prize for
Literature in 1948. His publications include *The Waste Land* (1922),
Murder in the Cathedral (1935) and a book of light verse, *Old
Possum's Book of Practical Cats* (1939).

ELEANOR FARJEON (1881-1965) was born in London. She wrote
stories and poems for children and published more than eighty
books. Among the best known are *Kings and Queens* (1932), written

in collaboration with her brother Herbert, and *The Little Bookroom* (1955).

MAX FATCHEN was born in 1920 near Adelaide, Australia. He has written several stories for young readers inspired by the sea and by his travels in the outback and along Australia's rivers. His poetry for children includes *Songs for My Dog and Other People* (1980) and *Wry Rhymes for Troublesome Times* (1983).

RACHEL FIELD (1894-1942) was born in New York City. One of her novels for adults, *All This and Heaven Too* (1938), became a successful film. But she is best remembered for her children's story *Hitty, Her First Hundred Years* (1929) and for her collection of children's verse *Taxis and Toadstools* (1926).

ROBERT FROST (1874-1963) was born in San Francisco. He spent most of his life in New England and his poetry, collected in *The Poetry of Robert Frost* (1969), is closely associated with its landscape. In later life he was a friend of President Kennedy and read a poem at his Inauguration.

JOHN FULLER was born in 1937 in Kent. He is a Fellow of Magdalen College, Oxford. His novel *Flying to Nowhere* won the Whitbread Prize in 1983. Among his poetry publications are *Selected Poems* (1985) and, for children, *Squeaking Crust* (1974) and *Come Aboard and Sail Away* (1983).

MARY GILMORE (1865-1962) was born in New South Wales, Australia. She was a teacher, a journalist and a crusading trade-unionist. She published several collections of poems for adults, including *The Passionate Heart* (1918) and *Fourteen Men* (1954).

HARRY GRAHAM (1874-1936) was born in London. He was a captain in the Coldstream Guards. He wrote light verse for adults. Poems from two of his books, *Ruthless Rhymes for Heartless Homes* (1899) and *More Ruthless Rhymes for Heartless Homes* (1930), have become favourites with children.

ROBERT GRAVES (1895-1985) was born in London. From 1929 he made Majorca his home. He published many collections of poems and was a prolific writer of books on classical subjects, including the novel *I, Claudius* (1934). His poetry for children includes *The Penny Fiddle* (1960) and *Ann of Highwood Hall* (1964).

THOMAS HARDY (1840-1928) spent most of his life in his native Dorset. Between 1871 and 1895 he published his novels of country life. Both *Tess of the d'Urbervilles* (1891) and *Jude the Obscure* (1895) provoked controversy, and thereafter he concentrated on poetry. *Wessex Poems* (1898) was followed by eight more collections.

SEAMUS HEANEY was born in 1939 in County Derry, Northern Ireland. He has since made his home in Dublin. In 1989 he was elected Professor of Poetry at Oxford. Publications include *New and Selected Poems: 1966–1987* (1990), *The Spirit Level* (1996) and *Opened Ground* (1998).

JOHN HEATH-STUBBS was born in 1918 in London. He was an English lecturer until 1973 and has taught at universities in Egypt and America. He became blind in the 1970s and now composes his poems in his head. Publications include *Collected Poems: 1943–1987* (1988) and, for young readers, *A Parliament of Birds* (1975).

ADRIAN HENRI was born in 1932 in Birkenhead. He is associated with the Liverpool Poets and was included in *The Mersey Sound: Penguin Modern Poets 10* (1967). He is also a painter. Publications for children include *The Phantom Lollipop Lady* (1986), *The Rhinestone Rhino and Other Poems* (1989), *Robocat* (1998) and *The World's Your Lobster* (1998).

OLIVER HERFORD (1863-1935) was born in Sheffield. He emigrated to the United States when he was nineteen and worked as an illustrator for *Life* and *Harper's Weekly*. He wrote humorous verse and his collections include *Rubaiyat of a Persian Kitten* (1904) and *A Little Book of Bones* (1906).

PHOEBE HESKETH was born in 1909 in Lancashire. She has worked as a freelance journalist and as a teacher and writer. Her poetry publications include *Netting the Sun: New and Collected Poems* (1989) and, for children, *A Song of Sunlight* (1974).

RUSSELL HOBAN was born in 1925 in Pennsylvania. Since 1969 he has lived in London. He has written a number of picture books, including *How Tom Beat Captain Najork and His Hired Sportsmen* (1974) which won the 1974 Whitbread Children's Book Award, and *The Dancing Tigers* (1979). His other work includes *The Mouse and His Child* (1967) and *The Trokeville Way* (1996).

MARY ANN HOBERMAN was born in 1930 in Connecticut. She writes stories and poems for children, and many of her books are illustrated by her husband, Norman Hoberman. Among her poetry publications are *All My Shoes Come in Twos* (1957), *Not Enough Beds for the Babies* (1965) and *Fathers, Mothers, Sisters, Brothers* (1991).

A. E. (ALFRED EDWARD) HOUSMAN (1859-1936) was born in Worcestershire, although it is neighbouring Shropshire that features in his poems. He was a notable classical scholar and in 1911 became Professor of Latin at Cambridge. *A Shropshire Lad* (1896) was followed by *Last Poems* (1922) and *More Poems* (1936).

LIBBY HOUSTON was born in 1941 in London. She has contributed poetry programmes to the BBC Schools series *Pictures in Your Mind* and has published one collection of children's poetry, *All Change*. Her adult collections include *Plain Clothes* (1971) and *At the Mercy* (1981).

TED HUGHES (1930-1998) was born in Yorkshire. He was married to Sylvia Plath until her death in 1963. His poetry for children includes *Season Songs* (1975) and *Moon-Bells and Other Poems* (1978), and he edited, with Seamus Heaney, *The Rattle Bag* (1982). He became Poet Laureate in 1984. Adult titles include *Tales from Ovid: Twenty-Four Passages from the 'Metamorphoses'* and *The Birthday Letters* both published in 1998.

ELIZABETH JENNINGS was born in 1926 in Lincolnshire. She worked at Oxford City Library and then as a publisher's reader. Since 1961 she has been a freelance writer. Her poetry publications include *Collected Poems: 1953–1985* (1986) and, for children, *The Secret Brother* (1969), *After the Ark* (1978) and *A Spell of Words* (1997).

JACKIE KAY was born in 1961 in Scotland. Although she now lives and works in London, her childhood in Glasgow has become the inspiration for many of her poems. Her first poem was printed in the *Morning Star* when she was 12 years old and her first collection of poems, *Two's Company* (1992), won the Signal Poetry Award in 1993. Her children's poetry collections also include *Three Has Gone* (1994) and *The Frog who Dreamt She was an Opera Singer* (1998).

RUDYARD KIPLING (1865–1936) was born in Bombay of English parents. From 1899 he lived most of his life in England as a full-time writer. He received the Nobel Prize for Literature in 1907. His classic books for children are *The Jungle Book* (1894), *Kim* (1901) and the *Just So Stories* (1902).

JAMES KIRKUP was born in 1923 in South Shields. He has lived abroad for many years and, since 1963, has taught English at universities in Japan. He has published plays, an autobiography and translations. His poetry collections include *The Prodigal Son: Poems 1956–1959* (1959), *The Body Servant: Poems of Exile* (1971) and *Measure of Time: Collected Longer Poems* (1997).

PHILIP LARKIN (1922–85) was born in Coventry. From 1955 he was Librarian at the University of Hull. He was associated with the Movement poets of the 1950s and published three acclaimed volumes of poems, *The Less Deceived* (1955), *The Whitsun Weddings* (1964) and *High Windows* (1974). *Collected Poems* appeared in 1988.

DENNIS LEE was born in 1939 in Toronto. He is a poet, editor and critic. He also writes for children and, from 1982 to 1986, was a songwriter for the television programme *Fraggle Rock*. His collections of children's poetry include *Alligator Pie* (1974) and *Jelly Belly* (1983). *Nightwatch* (1996) is one of his recent adult collections.

LAURIE LEE (1914–1997) was born in Gloucestershire. He was well known for his books of autobiography, *Cider with Rosie* (1959) and *As I Walked Out One Midsummer Morning* (1969). Three early volumes of poetry are reprinted in *Selected Poems* (1983).

VACHEL LINDSAY (1879–1931) was born in Illinois. He was a minstrel-poet who in his youth exchanged his poems for food and lodgings. A popular performer, he none the less died, poor and in ill health, by suicide. Publications include *The Tramp's Excuse and Other Poems* (1909) and *Going-to-the-Stars* (1926).

CHRISTOPHER LOGUE was born in 1926 in Portsmouth. He is an actor, playwright and screenwriter as well as a poet-performer. Poetry for children and adults is collected in *Ode to the Dodo: Poems 1953–1979* (1981). He has edited several anthologies, including *The Children's Book of Comic Verse* (1979).

EDWARD LOWBURY was born in 1913 in London. He is a doctor and worked in the field of medical research until his retirement. His collections of poems include *Time For Sale* (1961), *Apollo* (1990), *Mystic Bridge* (1997) and, for children, *Green Magic* (1972).

NORMAN MACCAIG (1910-1996) was born in Edinburgh. He worked as a teacher until 1970 and then held positions at the universities of Edinburgh and Stirling. His books of poems include *Riding Lights* (1955) and *Rings on a Tree* (1968). His *Collected Poems* appeared in 1985.

DAVID McCORD was born in 1897 in New York City. He edited the *Harvard Alumni Bulletin* from 1940 to 1946, and he has written books in the fields of education, art, medicine and history. His poetry for children includes *Far and Few* (1952) and *Mr Bidery's Spidery Garden* (1972).

ROGER McGOUGH was born in 1937 in Liverpool. He is one of the Liverpool Poets who appeared in *The Mersey Sound: Penguin Modern Poets 10* (1967). His poems often appeal equally to adults and to children. Publications include *In the Glassroom* (1976), *Selected Poems* (1989) and, specifically for children, *Sky in the Pie* (1983), *Pillow Talk* (1990) and *Bad, Bad Cats* (1997).

JOHN MASEFIELD (1878-1967) was born in Herefordshire. He was a sailor in his youth, and the sea features in the many ballads and narrative poems which he wrote. In 1930 he was appointed Poet Laureate. His books of poems include *Salt-Water Ballads* (1902) and *Reynard the Fox* (1919).

EVE MERRIAM was born in 1916 in New York City. She has worked on radio, as a teacher and in publishing. She writes for both adults and children. Among her poetry collections for the young are *There Is No Rhyme for Silver* (1962), *It Doesn't Always Have to Rhyme* (1964), *Higgle Wiggle: Happy Rhymes* (1994) and *You Be Good & I'll Be Night: Jump-On-The-Bed Poems* (1996).

SPIKE MILLIGAN was born in 1918 in India. He was a star of the *Goon Show*, a radio comedy famous from the 1950s, and is well known as a television personality. His humorous books for children include *Silly Verse for Kids* (1959), *Unspun Socks from a Chicken's Laundry* (1981) and *Startling Verse for All the Family* (1987). He was awarded an honorary CBE in 1992.

A. A. (ALAN ALEXANDER) MILNE (1882-1956) was born in London. He was a successful dramatist. But it is the books written for his son, Christopher Robin, that have become classics: *Winnie-the-Pooh* (1926), *The House at Pooh Corner* (1928) and, in verse, *When We Were Very Young* (1924) and *Now We Are Six* (1927).

ADRIAN MITCHELL was born in 1932 in London. He writes in various media for adults and children. *Love Songs of World War III* (1989) is a collection of lyrics from his plays and shows. Poetry publications include *For Beauty Douglas: Collected Poems 1953–1979* (1982) and, for children, *Nothingmas Day* (1984) and *Balloon Lagoon and the Magic Islands of Poetry* (1997).

EDWIN MORGAN was born in 1920 in Glasgow. From 1947 he taught at Glasgow University and was Professor of English there from 1975 to 1985. He has translated several Eastern European poets. Collections of his own poetry include *Selected Poems* (1985), *Themes on a Variation* (1988) and *Virtual and Other Realities* (1997).

PETER MORTIMER was born in 1943 in Nottingham. He is an editor of the literary magazine *Iron*. He has written poems for adults and has published two collections for children, *Utter Nonsense* (1977) and *Oosquidal* (1981).

OGDEN NASH (1902-1971) was born in New York State. He began as a serious poet but then turned, with spectacular success, to light verse. He published several books specifically for children, but adults and young readers alike enjoy the poems in such collections as *The Primrose Path* (1955).

GRACE NICHOLS was born in 1950 in Guyana. She worked there as a journalist and reporter, before coming to Britain in 1977 and has since published several books of poems for adults including *The Fat Black Woman's Poems* (1984), *Lazy Thoughts of a Lazy Woman* (1989) and *Sunris* (1996). Her children's poetry collections include *Give Yourself A Hug* (1994) and *No Hickory, No Dickory, No Dock* with John Agard (1996).

GARETH OWEN was born in 1936 in Lancashire. He has worked in theatre in Birmingham as an actor and director. His collections of poems for children include *Song of the City* (1985), *Salford Road and Other Poems* (1988), *My Granny is a Sumo Wrestler* (1994) and *The Fox on the Roundabout* (1995).

WILFRED OWEN (1893-1918) was born in Shropshire. He is regarded as the foremost poet of the First World War, during which he wrote his mature poetry. He was killed a week before the Armistice. *Poems* (1920) was edited by Siegfried Sassoon. *Collected Poems* appeared in 1963.

KENNETH PATCHEN (1911-1972) was born in Ohio. A graphic artist as well as a poet, he combined poems and drawings in numerous publications. He also performed his work to the accompaniment of jazz musicians. His copious output is represented in *Collected Poems* (1967).

A. B. (ANDREW BARTON) 'BANJO' PATERSON (1864-1941) was born in New South Wales, Australia. Although a qualified solicitor, he lived an adventurous life as war correspondent, newspaper editor and grazier. He published several books of popular ballads, including *The Man from Snowy River* (1895), and one book for children, *The Animals Noah Forgot* (1933).

MERVYN PEAKE (1911-1968) was born in China. He was a gifted artist and illustrator of children's books. His poetry for children includes *Rhymes Without Reason* (1944) and *A Book of Nonsense* (1972). His best-known work of fiction for adults is his 'Titus' trilogy, beginning with *Titus Groan* (1946).

LYDIA PENDER was born in 1907 in London. She has lived most of her life in Australia. She writes stories and poems for children.

Among her publications are *Barnaby and the Horses* (1961) and her collected poems for children, *Morning Magpie* (1984).

SYLVIA PLATH (1932–1963) was born in Boston, Massachusetts. She married Ted Hughes in 1956 while a student at Cambridge. They were separated at the time of her death by suicide. Most of her poetry appeared posthumously, including *Collected Poems* (1961), *Ariel* (1963) and, for children, *The Bed Book* (1976).

JACK PRELUTSKY was born in 1940 in New York City. He is author of more than thirty collections of children's poetry, including *The Queen of Eene* (1970), *Nightmares* (1976), *The New Kid on the Block* (1984), *The Dragons are Singing Tonight* (1993) and *A Pizza the Size of the Sun* (1996).

KATHARINE PYLE (1863–1938) was born in Delaware, where she lived in the family house at Wilmington until her death. Many of her poems were illustrated by her brother, Howard Pyle, himself a well-known children's writer. Publications include *Careless Jane and Other Tales* (1904) and *The Pearl Fairy Book* (1923).

KATHLEEN RAINE was born in 1908 in London. She is the author of several books on William Blake and other romantic poets. Her own poetry publications include *The Year One* (1932), *Collected Poems: 1935–1980* (1981) and *Living With Mystery* (1992).

JAMES REEVES (1909–78) was born in London. He edited and wrote many books on poets and poetry. He also wrote poems for adults but is best known for his children's verse. His publications include *How to Write Poems for Children* (1971) and *Complete Poems for Children* (1973).

LAURA E. RICHARDS (1850–1943) was born in Boston, Massachusetts, daughter of Julia Ward Howe. She wrote prolifically for adults and especially for children. She is best remembered nowadays for her children's poems, notably those in *Tirra Lirra: Rhymes Old and New* (1932).

E. V. (EMILE VICTOR) RIEU (1887–1972) was born in London. He was editor of Penguin Classics from 1944 to 1964 and himself translated *The Odyssey* (1946). He published two books of children's verse, *Cuckoo Calling: A Book of Verse for Youthful People* (1933) and *The Flattered Flying Fish and Other Poems* (1962).

THEODORE ROETHKE (1908–63) was born in Michigan. From 1947 he taught at the University of Washington. His poems reflect his childhood intimacy with his father's greenhouses, notably in *The Lost Son* (1948). Other publications include his collected poems for children, *I Am! Says the Lamb* (1961).

MICHAEL ROSEN was born in 1946 in Harrow, Middlesex. He writes stories and poems for children. He is a popular performer of his work and a well-known advocate of children's books. He won the Eleanor Farjeon Award in 1997 for his contribution to children's literature. Poetry collections include *Mind Your Own Business* (1974), *Wouldn't You Like To Know* (1977), *Quick, Let's Get Out of Here* (1983) and *You Wait Till I'm Older Than You!* (1996).

A. L. (ALFRED LESLIE) ROWSE (1903–1997) was born in Cornwall, the setting for many of his poems and autobiographical books. He was an eminent historian and was a Fellow of All Souls College, Oxford, from 1925 to 1974. His *Collected Poems* appeared in 1981.

VERNON SCANNELL was born in 1922 in Lincolnshire. He was a boxer before becoming a teacher of English. Since 1962 he has been a full-time writer. His publications include *New and Collected Poems: 1950–1980* (1980) and, for children, *The Apple Raid and Other Poems* (1974) and *The Clever Potato* (1988). More poems for children appear in the anthology *We Couldn't Provide Fish Thumbs* (1997).

IAN SERRAILLIER (1912–1994) was born in London. He was a schoolmaster until 1961, after which he devoted his time to his children's writing. Publications include the poetry collection *Thomas and the Sparrow* (1946) and the novel *The Silver Sword* (1956), which has been serialized for television.

ROBERT SERVICE (1874–1958) was born in Preston and lived in Glasgow until he was twenty-one. He emigrated to western Canada and there began to write his popular ballads. These include *Songs of a Sourdough* (1907) and *Ballads of a Cheechako* (1909).

SHEL SILVERSTEIN was born in 1932 in Chicago. He is a cartoonist, composer and folk-singer as well as a children's poet. Among his publications are *Where the Sidewalk Ends* (1974), *A Light in the Attic* (1981) and *Falling Up: Poems and Drawings* (1996).

EDITH SITWELL (1887-1964) was born in Scarborough, Yorkshire. Her background was aristocratic but her own life was Bohemian. She edited the avant-garde magazine *Wheels* and gave celebrated performances of her poems. Publications include *Façade* (1922), which was set to music by William Walton, and *The Sleeping Beauty* (1924).

STEVIE SMITH (1902-71) was born in Hull. When she was three she moved to London with her family and lived in the same house until her death. Her poetry collections, each illustrated with her own drawings, include *Not Waving But Drowning* (1957) and *The Scorpion and Other Poems* (1972).

JAMES STEPHENS (1880-1950) was born in Dublin. He lived in obscure circumstances until he became known as a figure in the Irish literary revival. He wrote poems and translations from the Irish, but he is best remembered for the humorous prose-fantasy *The Crock of Gold* (1912).

DYLAN THOMAS (1914-53) was born in Swansea. He was the leading poet among the neo-Romantics of the 1940s. His early death, during a reading tour in America, was due largely to alcoholism. Publications include *Collected Poems* (1952) and a play for television and radio, *Under Milk Wood* (1954).

EDWARD THOMAS (1878-1917) was born in London. He was a freelance writer until, at the age of thirty-six, he met Robert Frost. He began to write poems and composed steadily until his death, three years later, in France at the Battle of Arras. *Collected Poems* appeared in 1920.

W. J. (WALTER JAMES) TURNER (1889-1946) was born in Melbourne, Australia. He moved to London when he was seventeen and worked as a music and drama critic. He wrote novels and published several collections of poetry, including *The Hunter and Other Poems* (1916) and *The Dark Fire* (1918).

JOHN WALSH (1911-72) was born in Brighton. He was an English teacher and wrote poems for children. His published work includes *The Roundabout by the Sea* (1960) and *The Truants and Other Poems for Children* (1965).

RICHARD WILBUR was born in 1921 in New York City. He has taught at Harvard and other universities in America, and in 1987 he became the American Poet Laureate. His publications include *New and Selected Poems* (1988) and, for children, *Loudmouse* (1963), *Opposites* (1973) and *The Disappearing Alphabet* (1998).

NANCY WILLARD was born in 1936 in Ann Arbor, Michigan. She writes for both children and adults. Among her publications for children are the storybook *Simple Pictures Are Best* (1977) and the poetry collections *A Visit to William Blake's Inn* (1981) and *An Alphabet of Angels* (1994).

RAYMOND WILSON (1925-1995) was born in Gateshead, County Durham. Until his retirement in 1989, he was Professor of Education at Reading University. He was a well-known anthologist of children's poetry. His publications include *Daft Davy: A Story in Verse* (1987) and, as editor, *Nine O'Clock Bell: Poems about School* (1985).

MARGARET WISE BROWN (1910-52) was born in New York City. She was a prolific writer of stories for children, including several under the pseudonym Golden MacDonald. Her poetry for children includes *The Dark Wood of the Golden Birds* (1950) and *Nibble Nibble* (1959).

JUDITH WRIGHT was born in 1915 in New South Wales, Australia. *The Moving Image: Poems* (1946) established her as an important Australian poet. She has published many collections since and has edited *A Book of Australian Verse* (1968). She has also written stories for children, including *King of the Dingoes* (1959). Her *Collected Poems* appeared in 1994.

KIT WRIGHT was born in 1944 in Kent. He taught at Brock University, Canada, for three years and has been a Fellow Commoner at Cambridge. His publications include *Poems 1974-1983* (1988) and, for children, *Hot Dog and Other Poems* (1981), *Cat Among the Pigeons* (1987) and *Great Snakes!* (1994).

W. B. (WILLIAM BUTLER) YEATS (1865-1939) was born in Dublin. He was the leading figure of the Irish literary revival and a founder of the Abbey Theatre. He served for six years in the Irish Senate. In 1923 he received the Nobel Prize for Literature. *Collected Poems* appeared in 1950.

BENJAMIN ZEPHANIAH was born in 1958 in Birmingham. He spent some of his early years in Jamaica which has had a dramatic effect on his work. He is well-known for his 'rap' style making his poetry highly accessible and very modern. His publications include *City Psalms* (1992) and *Propa Propaganda* (1996) and, for children, *Talking Turkeys* (1994) and *Funky Chickens* (1996).

ACKNOWLEDGEMENTS

The editor and publishers gratefully acknowledge permission to reproduce copyright material in this book:

By kind permission of John Agard c/o Caroline Sheldon Literary Agency 'Hatch Me a Riddle' and 'Laughter's Chant' from *Laughter is an Egg* (Penguin, 1990), 'Limbo Dancer's Soundpoem' from *Limbo Dancer in Dark Glasses* (Greenheart, 1983) and 'Don't Call Alligator Long-Mouth Till You Cross River' from *Say It Again* (Bodley Head, 1985); 'I Did a Bad Thing Once' and 'The Cane' by Allan Ahlberg reprinted from *Please Mrs Butler* (Viking Kestrel, 1983) copyright © Allan Ahlberg, 1983 and 'Billy McBone' by Allan Ahlberg reprinted from *Heard it in the Playground* (Viking Kestrel, 1989) copyright © Allan Ahlberg, 1989 by permission of Penguin Books Ltd; 'Night Mail' by W. H. Auden reprinted from *Collected Shorter Poems* by permission of Faber & Faber Ltd; 'Elephant' by George Barker reprinted from *The Alphabetical Zoo*, 'I Never See the Stars at Night' by George Barker reprinted from *To Aylsham Fair* and 'They Call to One Another' by George Barker reprinted from *Collected Poems* all by permission of Faber & Faber Ltd; 'The Frog', 'Jack and His Pony, Tom', 'The Microbe', 'Rebecca' and 'The Vulture' by Hilaire Belloc reprinted from *The Complete Verse of Hilaire Belloc* by permission of Peters Fraser & Dunlop Group Ltd; 'Dreaming Black Boy' and 'A Story About Afiya' by James Berry, copyright © James Berry, 1988 reprinted from *When I Dance* (Hamish Hamilton, 1988) by permission of Hamish Hamilton Children's Books; 'Diary of a Church Mouse' by John Betjeman reprinted from *Church Poems* by permission of John Murray (Publishers) Ltd; 'John' and 'Perfect Arthur' by N. M. Bodecker by permission of Macmillan Inc.; 'In Daylight Strange' by Alan Brownjohn, copyright © Alan Brownjohn, 1970 by permission of the author and 'Parrot' by Alan Brownjohn reprinted from *Brownjohn's*

Beasts by permission of Macmillan, London and Basingstoke; 'Lord of the Dance' by Sydney Carter, copyright © Stainer and Bell Ltd, 1963 reprinted by permission of Stainer and Bell Ltd; 'Colonel Fazackerley', 'The Forest of Tangle', 'Timothy Winters', 'Tom Bone' and 'Who?' by Charles Causley reprinted from *Collected Poems* by permission of David Higham Associates Ltd; 'Good Company' by Leonard Clark reprinted from *Good Company* (Dobson Books) by permission of Dobson Books Ltd and 'The Singing Time' by Leonard Clark, copyright © The Literary Executor of Leonard Clark, 1977 by permission of The Literary Executor of Leonard Clark; 'Song of the Rabbits Outside the Tavern' by Elizabeth Coatsworth reprinted from *Country Poems* (Macmillan Inc. 1942) by permission of Catherine Beston Barnes; 'in Just-', 'little tree' and 'maggie and milly and molly and may' by e. e. cummings reprinted from *Selected Poems* by permission of HarperCollins Ltd; 'Down Vith Children! Do Them In!' by Roald Dahl reprinted from *The Witches* (Jonathan Cape and Penguin Books) by permission of Murray Pollinger; 'Before Dawn', 'The Linnet', 'The Listeners', 'A Robin', 'The Scarecrow' and 'Tom's Angel' by Walter de la Mare reprinted from *Collected Poems* by permission of The Literary Trustees of Walter de la Mare and The Society of Authors as their representative; 'Billy' and 'Nightening' by Michael Dugan reprinted from *Flocks, Socks and Other Shocks* by permission of Penguin Books Australia Ltd and 'Obsequious Prawn' by Michael Dugan, copyright © Michael Dugan, 1974 reprinted from *Stuff and Nonsense* (William Collins, Australia, 1974) by permission of the author; 'The Lion and Albert' by Marriott Edgar, copyright © 1933 reprinted by permission of Francis, Day and Hunter Ltd; 'Littlemouse', 'When I Was Three' and 'The Word Party' by Richard Edwards, copyright © Richard Edwards, 1986 reprinted from *The Word Party* (Lutterworth Press, 1986) by permission of the Lutterworth Press and 'Me and Him' by Richard Edwards reprinted from A *Mouse in My Roof* (Orchard Books, 1988) by permission of Orchard Books; 'Skimbleshanks: The Railway Cat' by T. S. Eliot reprinted from *Old Possum's Book of Practical Cats* by permission of Faber & Faber Ltd; 'The Distance', 'Mrs Malone' and 'The Night Will Never Stay' by Eleanor Farjeon, copyright © Gervase Farjeon, 1951 reprinted from *Silver-Sand and Snow* (Michael Joseph, 1951) and 'The Sounds in the Evening', by Eleanor Farjeon reprinted from *Invitation to a Mouse* (Hodder and Stoughton) all by permission of

David Higham Associates Ltd; 'Just Fancy That' and an extract from 'Ruinous Rhymes' by Max Fatchen, copyright © Max Fatchen, 1983 reprinted from *Wry Rhymes for Troublesome Times* (Kestrel Books, 1983) by permission of Penguin Books Ltd; 'Something Told the Wild Geese' by Rachel Field reprinted from *Poems* (Macmillan) by permission of Macmillan Publishing Company; 'The Last Word of a Bluebird', 'A Minor Bird' and 'Stopping by Woods on a Snowy Evening' by Robert Frost, reprinted from *The Poetry of Robert Frost* by permission of Jonathan Cape and the Estate of Robert Frost; 'Creatures' and 'Lock-Out in Eden' by John Fuller reprinted from *Come Aboard and Sail Away* (Salamander Press, 1983) and 'Funeral March' by John Fuller reprinted from *Squeaking Crust* (Chatto and Windus, 1974) by permission of the author; 'The Wild Horses' by Mary Gilmore copyright © The Estate of Dame Mary Gilmore, reprinted by permission of Collins/Angus & Robertson Publishers; 'The *Alice Jean*', 'The Penny Fiddle', 'The Six Badgers' and 'Welsh Incident' by Robert Graves reprinted from *The Penny Fiddle* by permission of A. P. Watt Ltd on behalf of The Trustees of the Robert Graves Copyright Trust; 'Mid-Term Break' by Seamus Heaney reprinted from *Death of a Naturalist* by permission of Faber & Faber Ltd; 'The Kingfisher' by John Heath-Stubbs reprinted from A *Charm Against Toothache* by permission of David Higham Associates Ltd; 'Best Friends' by Adrian Henri, copyright © Adrian Henri, 1986 reprinted from *The Phantom Lollipop Lady* (Methuen, 1986) and 'Tonight at Noon' by Adrian Henri, copyright © Adrian Henri, 1986 reprinted from *Tonight at Noon* (Allison & Busby) both by permission of Rogers, Coleridge & White Ltd; 'Truant' by Phoebe Hesketh reprinted from *No Time for Cowards* (Heinemann, 1952) by permission of the author; 'Funeral' by Russell Hoban reprinted from *Six of the Best* by permission of David Higham Associates Ltd; 'Combinations' by Mary Ann Hoberman, reprinted from *Bugs* (Viking, 1976), copyright © Mary Ann Hoberman, 1976, 'Brother' by Mary Ann Hoberman, copyright © Mary Ann Hoberman, 1959, renewed 1987, reprinted from *Hello and Goodbye* (Little Brown, 1959) and 'Whale' by Mary Ann Hoberman, copyright © Mary Ann Hoberman, 1973 reprinted from A *Raucous Ark* (Viking, 1973) by permission of Gina Maccoby Literary Agency; 'The Dream of the Cabbage Caterpillars' and 'Talk About Caves' by Libby Houston, copyright © Libby Houston, 1973, 1983 reprinted from *Pictures in Your Mind* (BBC, 1973, 1983) and

'The Old Woman and the Sandwiches' by Libby Houston, copyright © Libby Houston, 1971 reprinted from *Plain Clothes* (Allison and Busby, 1971) all by permission of the author; 'Amulet' and 'Horrible Song' by Ted Hughes reprinted from *Moon Bells and Other Poems* (Chatto & Windus, 1970) by permission of Olwyn Hughes, 'Leaves' and 'Snow and Snow' by Ted Hughes reprinted from *Season Songs* and 'My Other Granny' reprinted from *Meet My Folks!* by permission of Faber & Faber Ltd; 'The Rabbit's Advice' by Elizabeth Jennings, copyright © Elizabeth Jennings, 1978 reprinted from *After the Ark* (Oxford University Press, 1978), 'Lullaby' and 'The Secret Brother' by Elizabeth Jennings, copyright © Elizabeth Jennings, 1966 reprinted from *The Secret Brother* (Macmillan, 1966) all by permission of David Higham Associates Ltd; 'The Frog Who Dreamed She Was an Opera Singer' and 'Word of a Lie' by Jackie Kay, copyright © Jackie Kay, 1998 reprinted from *The Frog Who Dreamed She Was an Opera Singer* (Bloomsbury Children's Books, 1998) by permission of Bloomsbury Children's Books; 'The Kitten in the Falling Snow' by James Kirkup by permission of the author; 'Cut Grass' by Philip Larkin reprinted from *High Windows,* 'Take One Home for the Kiddies' by Philip Larkin reprinted from *The Whitsun Weddings* by permission of Faber & Faber Ltd; 'Lizzy's Lion' by Dennis Lee, copyright © Dennis Lee by permission of McKnight Gosewich Associates Agency Inc.; 'Apples' by Laurie Lee, copyright © Laurie Lee, 1983 reprinted from *Selected Poems* (André Deutsch, 1983) by permission of André Deutsch Ltd; 'The Ass's Song' by Christopher Logue reprinted from *Ode to the Dodo* by permission of Jonathan Cape; 'The Huntsman' by Edward Lowbury reprinted from *Time for Sale* (Chatto & Windus, 1961) by permission of the Hippopotamus Press; 'Blind Horse' and 'Frogs' by Norman MacCaig reprinted from *Collected Poems* by permission of Chatto & Windus; 'Glowworm' and 'Pad and Pencil' by David McCord, copyright © David McCord, 1961, 1962, 1965 reprinted from *Every Time I Climb a Tree* by permission of Little, Brown and Company; 'Three Rusty Nails' and 'Streemin' by Roger McGough reprinted from *In The Glassroom* by permission of Jonathan Cape, 'The Identification' by Roger McGough reprinted from *New Volume,* 'Sky in the Pie!' by Roger McGough reprinted from *Sky in the Pie* (Kestrel, 1983), copyright © Roger McGough, 1983 and 'Slug' by Roger McGough reprinted from *An Imaginary Menagerie* by permission of Peters, Fraser & Dunlop Group Ltd; 'An Old Song Re-Sung' and

'Roadways' by John Masefield by permission of The Society of Authors as the literary representative of the Estate of John Masefield; 'Catch a Little Rhyme' by Eve Merriam, copyright © Eve Merriam, 1966 by permission of Marian Reiner for the author; 'The ABC' and 'Today I Saw a Little Worm' by Spike Milligan reprinted from *Silly Verse For Kids*, 'Lady B's Fleas' by Spike Milligan reprinted from *A Dustbin of Milligan*, 'The "Veggy" Lion' and 'The Ying-tong-iddle-I-po' by Spike Milligan reprinted from *Unspun Socks From a Chicken's Laundry* all by permission of Spike Milligan Productions Ltd; 'Daffodowndilly', 'Lines and Squares' by A. A. Milne reprinted from *When We Were Very Young* (Methuen Children's Books) and 'Waiting at the Window' by A. A. Milne reprinted from *Now We Are Six* (Methuen Children's Books) by permission of the Octopus Publishing Group; 'Dumb Insolence', 'The Galactic Pachyderm', 'Stufferation' and 'The Woman of Water' by Adrian Mitchell, copyright © Adrian Mitchell, 1964 reprinted from *Nothingmas Day* (Allison and Busby, 1964) by permission of the author; 'The Computer's First Christmas Card' by Edwin Morgan reprinted from *Collected Poems* by permission of Carcanet Press Ltd; 'Babies are Boring' by Peter Mortimer, copyright © Peter Mortimer, 1983 reprinted from *Utter Nonsense* (Iron Press, 1986) by permission of the author; 'Adventures of Isabel', 'The Parent' and 'The Purist' by Ogden Nash reprinted from *Candy is Dandy* and 'The Wombat' by Ogden Nash first published by *Saturday Evening Post* all by permission of Curtis Brown Ltd; 'A-ra-rat' by Grace Nichols reprinted from *No Hickory No Dickory No Dock* (Viking, 1991) copyright © Grace Nichols 1991 and 'I Like to Stay Up' by Grace Nichols reprinted from *Come On Into My Tropical Garden* (A & C Black, 1988) copyright © Grace Nichols 1988 both by permission of Curtis Brown Ltd, London, on behalf of Grace Nichols; 'Dear Mr Examiner' by Gareth Owen reprinted from *Salford Road and Other Poems* (Glasgow: Young Lions, 1988) by permission of Rogers, Coleridge & White and 'Shed in Space' by Gareth Owen reprinted from *Shed in Space* by permission of HarperCollins Publishers Ltd; 'The Magical Mouse' by Kenneth Patchen reprinted from *Collected Poems of Kenneth Patchen,* copyright © Kenneth Patchen, 1952 by permission of New Directions Publishing Corporation; 'I've Never Heard the Queen Sneeze', 'The Newcomer', 'Squeezes' and 'The Trouble With My Sister' by Brian Patten, copyright © Brian Patten, 1985 reprinted from *Gargling with Jelly* (Viking

Kestrel, 1985) by permission of Penguin Books Ltd; 'Aunts and Uncles', 'Little Spider', 'O Here It Is! And There It Is!', 'O'er Seas That Have No Beaches' and 'The Trouble with Geraniums' by Mervyn Peake copyright © The Estate of Mervyn Peake reprinted from *A Book of Nonsense* by permission of David Higham Associates Ltd; 'Giants' and 'The Lizard' by Lydia Pender copyright © Lydia Pender, 1984 reprinted from *Morning Magpie* by permission of Angus and Robertson Publishers Ltd; an extract from 'The Bed Book' by Sylvia Plath reprinted from *The Bed Book* by permission of Faber & Faber Ltd; 'Homework! Oh, Homework!' and 'Today is Very Boring' by Jack Prelutsky, copyright © Jack Prelutsky reprinted from *New Kid on the Block* (Greenwillow Books) and 'Huffer and Cuffer' by Jack Prelutsky, copyright © Jack Prelutsky, 1982 reprinted from *The Sheriff of Rottenshot* (William Morrow) by permission of William Morrow & Co. Inc. and William Heinemann Ltd; 'Spell of Creation' by Kathleen Raine reprinted from *Collected Poems* by permission of Hamish Hamilton; 'The Intruder', 'Rabbit and Lark', 'Spells', 'Trees in the Moonlight' and 'W' by James Reeves reprinted from *The Wandering Moon and Other Poems* (Puffin Books) by permission of The James Reeves Estate; 'The Princess Priscilla', 'Rendezvous with a Beetle' and 'Sir Smashum Uppe' by E. V. Rieu reprinted from *Cuckoo Calling* (Methuen, 1933) by permission of Richard Rieu; 'My Papa's Waltz', 'The Serpent' and 'The Sloth' by Theodore Roethke reprinted from *The Collected Poems of Theodore Roethke* by permission of Faber & Faber Ltd; 'I Know Someone Who Can' by Michael Rosen reprinted from *Quick Let's Get Out of Here,* 'I'm the Youngest in Our House' and 'If You Don't Put Your Shoes On Before I Count Fifteen' by Michael Rosen reprinted from *You Can't Catch Me* all by permission of André Deutsch and 'When You're a Grown-Up' by Michael Rosen, copyright © Michael Rosen, 1979 reprinted from *You Tell Me* by Roger McGough and Michael Rosen (Kestrel Books, 1979) by permission of Penguin Books Ltd; 'The White Cat of Trenarren' by A. L. Rowse reprinted by permission of the author; 'The Apple-Raid' by Vernon Scannell reprinted from *The Apple-Raid and Other Poems* by permission of The Bodley Head and 'Growing Pain' by Vernon Scannell reprinted from *New and Collected Poems* (Robson Books, 1980) by permission of Robson Books Ltd; 'The Crooked Man' and 'The Visitor' by Ian Serraillier by permission of the author; 'The Cremation of Sam McGee' and 'Old David Smail' by Robert Service reprinted from *Collected Poems* (Dodd Mead & Company,

1916) by permission of The Estate of Robert Service; 'The Generals', 'Jimmy Jet and His TV Set' and 'Sick' by Shel Silverstein reprinted from *Where the Sidewalk Ends* by permission of HarperCollins Publishers and Jonathan Cape; 'Aubade' and 'Song XV *from* The Sleeping Beauty' by Edith Sitwell reprinted from *Façade and Other Poems* by permission of Duckworth; 'The Frog Prince' and 'The Old Sweet Dove of Wiveton' by Stevie Smith by permission of James MacGibbon; 'The Song of the Mischievous Dog' by Dylan Thomas reprinted from *The Poems* by permission of David Higham Associates Ltd; 'India' by W. J. Turner by permission of Sidgwick and Jackson; 'The Bully Asleep' by John Walsh reprinted from *Poets in Hand* (Puffin, 1998) by permission of Mrs A. M. Walsh; 'Some Opposites' by Richard Wilbur, copyright © Richard Wilbur, 1973 reprinted from *Opposites* by permission of Harcourt Brace Jovanovich Inc.; 'Blake Leads a Walk on the Milky Way' and 'A Rabbit Reveals My Room' by Nancy Willard, copyright © Nancy Willard, 1981 reprinted from A *Visit to William Blake's Inn: Poems for Innocent and Experienced Travellers* by permission of Harcourt Brace Jovanovich Inc.; 'Never Since Eden' by Raymond Wilson, copyright © Raymond Wilson by permission of the author; 'Full Moon Rhyme' and 'Magpies' by Judith Wright copyright © Judith Wright reprinted from *Collected Poems* by permission of Collins/Angus & Robertson Publishers; 'Hugger Mugger', 'Hundreds and Thousands' and 'Laurie and Dorrie' by Kit Wright copyright © Kit Wright, 1981 reprinted from *Hot Dog and Other Poems* (Kestrel Books, 1981) and 'Just Before Christmas' by Kit Wright, copyright © Kit Wright, 1987 reprinted from *Cat Among the Pigeons* (Viking Kestrel, 1987) by permission of Penguin Books Ltd. 'The Song of the Wandering Aengus' by W. B. Yeats from *The Collected Poems of W. B. Yeats*, reprinted by permission of A. P. Watt Ltd on behalf of Michael Yeats; 'Body Talk' by Benjamin Zephaniah from *Talking Turkeys*, published by Viking 1994, copyright © Benjamin Zephaniah, 1994, and 'This Orange Tree' by Benjamin Zephaniah from *Funky Chickens*, published by Viking 1996, copyright © Benjamin Zephaniah, 1996, both reprinted by permission of Penguin Books Ltd.

Every effort has been made to trace copyright holders, but in a few cases this has proved impossible. The editor and publishers apologize for these unwilling cases of copyright transgression and would like to hear from any copyright holders not acknowledged.